RED LETTER DAYS

Also by the same authors

TIME TO ACT
LIGHTNING SKETCHES

RED LETTER DAYS

Paul Burbridge
and
Murray Watts

HODDER AND STOUGHTON
LONDON SYDNEY AUCKLAND TORONTO

British Library Cataloguing in Publication Data

Burbridge, Paul
  Red letter days.
  1. Church year
  I. Title   II. Watts, Murray
  263'.9   BV30

  ISBN 0 340 38347 X

*To the memory of David Watson,
his friendship and inspiration.*

Red Letter Day: *A lucky day; a day to be recalled with delight. In almanacs, and more commonly in ecclesiastical calendars, important feast days and saints' days are printed in red, other days in black.*

Brewer's Dictionary of Phrase and Fable

FOREWORD

This is a wonderful book, full of laughter and surprises. It reminds me of one of those Advent calendars with little windows to open up for every day leading to Christmas – only this book starts with Christmas and goes through the whole year.

As an entertainer myself, I enjoy being entertained by somebody else and this book has kept me laughing. It has also made me think, too. The authors are good at that and I gladly accepted when they asked me to become a patron of Riding Lights Theatre Company some years ago. I have always admired the company's ability to combine first-rate entertainment with a challenge to their audience. This is true not only of the sketches in this book but also of their plays, so it's good to see the article at the end, describing the more ambitious work of the company.

A few years ago, I introduced a film of a Riding Lights production for Yorkshire Television and saw for myself their high standards of professionalism and their ability to touch audiences. In its own way, each of these twenty-six sketches here has something of that quality, whether it is funny or sad, poignant or highly provocative. They all have something to say and together they make up a treasury of material for groups all over the country and – if their other books are anything to go by – all over the world as well.

I commend this book to you all, and hope that you have a lot of fun and satisfaction both reading it and performing the sketches.

Roy Castle

LICENCE TO PERFORM THE SKETCHES IN THIS VOLUME

Any performance of a sketch in this book must be given under licence. This is in accordance with the procedure relating to all published theatrical work. Permission from the copyright holder would normally be granted for a specific performance but, as with our other books, we have decided to continue the policy of issuing a licence covering all the material in *Red Letter Days* for a fixed fee.

1. A licence for *Red Letter Days* costs £20.00.
2. It will be issued in the name of the group or individual intending to present the material. Licences are not transferable.
3. It guarantees the right to perform all the sketches for a period of *five years*, as often as the licensee wishes. (We cannot make exceptions for 'one-off' performances of a single sketch but hope that the purchase of a licence will encourage fuller use of the material.)
4. It does *not* confer the right to reproduce the text in any form. (See the copyright note on p. 4.)
5. Acknowledgments at any performance should mention the title, authors and publisher.
6. All cassette recording, radio, television, video and film rights are reserved.

Licence applications should be sent to: Red Letter Days, P.O. Box 223, York, YO1 1GW.

All cheques and money orders should be made payable to '*Red Letter Days*'.

Please note that applications for licences for other books by the authors should be made on separate cheques and sent to the title and address specified in each book.

The above refers to amateur productions (with paying or non-paying audiences). A separate application should be made to the same address by any fully professional company wishing to perform this material. Agreement will involve the payment of royalties on box-office takings.

CONTENTS

INTRODUCTION

ONE: That's it, then.

TWO: What?

ONE: The book. Finished.

TWO: Yes. Marvellous. (*Pause*) Shall I begin, then?

ONE: What?

TWO: The introduction.

ONE: I thought we weren't having one.

TWO: Well, not a full-blown, 'Hello-this-is-an-introduction', so much as a few words of . . .

ONE: Introduction.

TWO: 'Red Letter Days' . . . Special occasions, nice red print in the diary, the excitement of festivals throughout the year – it says it all.

ONE: Why do we need an introduction, then?

TWO: Okay. It doesn't say it *all*. That's why we need an introduction, get it?

ONE: Okay, okay, I was just asking. Carry on.

TWO: There is something for everybody in this book.

ONE: What, even for Melanesian Frog-worshippers?

TWO: Don't be childish.

ONE: You never know.

TWO: What?

ONE: Perhaps we should have included a sketch on the plague of frogs just in case. 'The Nile shall swarm with frogs which shall come up into your house, and into your bedchamber and on your bed, and into the house of your servants and of your people, and into your ovens and your kneading bowls.' It's very dramatic.

TWO: This book is about the Christian year.

ONE: Yes, yes, I know that.

TWO: Well, bearing that rather obvious fact in mind, we don't need to bother with frog-worshippers, locust-fondlers, or any other minority religious practices, do we?

ONE: No, you're right.

TWO: We can leave all that to Channel Four.

ONE: Good idea.

TWO: We've got quite enough work here in satisfying all the different Christian denominations.

ONE: So not the frogs this time, then?

TWO: No.

ONE: Pity. I really like the bit about the 'kneading bowls'. It's a graphic story.

TWO: As plagues go, it's a good one, yes.

ONE: And it's got good comic potential. 'Oven-ready frogs'.

TWO: LOOK. Can we just get on with describing this book?

ONE: Sorry. Go ahead.

TWO: This book is, essentially –

ONE: Isn't it rather superfluous to describe a book in the introduction?

TWO: All I'm doing is telling people what it's about, for heaven's sake.

ONE: Can't they just read it?

TWO: They might not 'just read it'. They might just, you never know, pick it up, thumb through a couple of pages, yawn, and pop it back on to the shelf. If we fail to *grab* their attention.

ONE: It's that bad, is it?

TWO: What?

ONE: The book, that we have to resort to grabbing people and forcing them to buy it.

TWO: All I'm saying is, we owe them some sort of introduction.

ONE: What, like putting a thundering great label under Constable's *Haywain*, saying, 'This is a nice picture of a country scene, with water, trees, a horse and a cart'?

TWO: You're trying my patience.

ONE: Not as much as you're trying the reader's patience with wild claims about 'something for everybody', when quite clearly vast sections of humanity are missed out, and, not content with that, rabbiting on about sketches which they are perfectly capable of reading for themselves.

TWO: Have you finished?

ONE: I was hoping you had.

TWO: All right, so there aren't sketches for everybody, but there are sketches for *every* occasion – nearly, nearly – every occasion in the Christian year.

ONE: One thing bothers me, though.

TWO: Just the one? I'm glad about that.

ONE: It's all rather heavy and high church, isn't it, this liturgical stuff? 'Advent', 'Trinity Sunday', 'All Saints' Day'. I mean, what about the free church chappies?

TWO: Don't patronise the free church, mate. You're talking to someone whose father was a Baptist, whose mother was Plymouth Brethren, who was brought

up in the Scottish Presbyterian Church,
who was confirmed an Anglican, and
married a Methodist.

ONE: Good grief, what does that make you?

TWO: Extremely confused. But that's not the
point. I can tell you from experience
that all these festivals are equally
relevant to Christians of every
persuasion. They are about the common
ground we all share, the very essence of
our faith.

ONE: Well put, I must say. Eloquent, pithy,
plausible. Have you ever thought of
selling pogo-sticks to kangaroos?

TWO: (*Oblivious*) Advent and Christmas, all
the way through to Easter and
Pentecost, not forgetting special events
like Mothering Sunday, or even a folk
festival like Guy Fawkes Night, and –

ONE: Hold it, hold it. I detect an introduction
here.

TWO: Sorry. I was just –

ONE: Describing the book.

TWO: Yes.

ONE: Furtively and rather dishonestly, if I
may say so.

TWO: Look, please, let me just say a couple of
words to the potential reader.

ONE: Listen, if he's got this far already, the
bookshop manager's going to get nasty.

TWO: So you think the potential reader has
either bought it by this point, or has, in
fact, replaced it on the shelf?

ONE: Exactly.

TWO: And so it would be quite redundant for
me to say that this book is an ideal
present for –

ONE: Oh, for goodness' sake.

TWO: Christmas, birthday or –

ONE: Trinity Sunday?

TWO: Er . . .

ONE: Mothering Sunday?

TWO: Possibly.

ONE: Harvest Thanksgiving?

TWO: Why not?

ONE: You think the poor and needy would prefer a copy of *Red Letter Days* to a corn on the cob?

TWO: All right, so it isn't an ideal present for every occasion, but it is *every* occasion for . . .

ONE: An ideal present?

TWO: That doesn't work. How about, 'every occasion in the church's year'?

ONE: Nearly.

TWO: Nearly every occasion.

ONE: 'Occasional Sketches'.

TWO: Careful. People might only perform them occasionally.

ONE: I thought you were used to that, with your sketches?

TWO: Very funny.

ONE: Anyway, we're agreed on one thing.

TWO: What?

ONE: No introduction, then.

TWO: Okay.

ONE: Just the sketches.

TWO: Right. Just the sketches, which cover practically every important occasion in the Christian year, are equally relevant to Christians of all denominations, expressing the major themes of historic Christianity but none the less being entirely relevant to an up-to-the-minute contemporary faith, and ideal for use by churches, schools, youth clubs, colleges, theatre companies and a wide variety of groups, not only in this country, but all over the world. Just the sketches. Right.

*Paul Burbridge and
Murray Watts*
York 1986

ADVENT AND CHRISTMAS

The First Coming

The very word 'Christmas' conjures up a thousand conflicting images. For children it means weeks of eager
anticipation, whereas for parents it may mean weeks of
clutching wallets with sweaty palms. For many people it
may mean a wonderful family reunion, whereas for the
hapless organiser of Christmas Dinner it may mean a
nervous breakdown at the sheer complexity of the social
dynamics – will Grandad and Aunty declare a truce? Will
Kevin be nicer to Granny's little doggy? Will Charlotte shut
up and eat what she is given? As for television stars, their
appearance on Christmas night is the climax of a successful
year, whereas for the unemployed actor – one of the most
poignant victims of Christmas – the 'season of good cheer'
may mean donning a silly red costume and pretending to be
extremely jolly for eight weeks in a stuffy department store.
Yet, despite all the conflicting emotions, the party hats,
crackers and festive spirit usually win the day, although
leaving people little the wiser about the true meaning of
'Christmas'.

It has, in fact, become a national habit to let the word
'Christmas' slip off the tongue without reflecting for a
moment on its origin (from the Old English 'Christes
Maesse' meaning 'the Mass of Christ'). The baby Jesus is
easily lost from sight in a forest of tinsel and paper chains,
and the true meaning of the Incarnation is well hidden
in the glowing cribs of sentimental Christmas cards. How
can we recover something of that awesome event in our
festivities?

Perhaps we can find a clue in the earliest celebrations of

Christmas. Nothing is known of any 'Christmas Day' before the fourth century in Rome, when it is likely that the decision to commemorate the birth of Christ – as well as His death and resurrection at Easter – had a lot to do with taking over a pagan festival and giving it new meaning. In AD 274, the Roman Emperor Aurelius had declared that the winter solstice – December 25th – should be a special feast day, the 'Dies Natalis Solis Invicti' (the birthday of the invincible sun). On that day the Sun-god began his return to Northern skies. This cult of sun worship was a rival to the growth of the Christian faith in Rome at the end of the third century, and Christians preached that Christ was the true 'sun' of righteousness, rising to bring light to the world. The evidence suggests that, with the victory of Christianity over the pagen religion, the early Church did not polarise the public by introducing new festivals, as much as take over the old and invest them with an entirely new significance.

Ironically, it could be said that the Church faces the same situation today: Christmas itself has become very largely a pagan festival, mixed up with end-of-the-year parties and folk customs. To turn our modern Christmas into a real celebration of the mystery of Incarnation, with all the implications of poverty, suffering, and glorious redemption of the world at Calvary, is an even more difficult task than the one faced by the early Christians. The contemporary Church suffers from a society which has been innoculated against the true meaning of Christmas by receiving a tiny dose of the real thing. We need to restore the meaning in every possible way and one way is to dramatise the events, making them come alive in the twentieth century.

The first two sketches for Advent* and Christmas take a look at the events in Bethlehem before there were any Christmas traditions. The other two look at Christmas in

---

* For a full discussion of Advent, see the last section in the book, p. 189.

the twentieth century: the first, 'The God Slot', at the way that meaning can be edited out of the festival, and the second, 'Getting Ready', at the way the 'Christmas rush' does anything but prepare us spiritually for the occasion.

The Two Shepherds

THE ARCHANGEL GABRIEL; SHENKYN, *a young shepherd*; LEWIN, *a senior shepherd in his late forties*

This scene has often been performed by Riding Lights Theatre Company as a sketch in its own right. It is in fact an extract from a full-length Christmas play called, The Tree That Woke Up, *which was first performed in 1975 by the Upstream Theatre Company at the Roses Theatre, Tewkesbury. It is a piece which will appeal to all ages – a modern expression of the old Mystery Play tradition where the sublime majesty of the Incarnation is mingled with the simple comedy of everyday life. As the Mystery Plays demonstrate, the comedy is not a frivolous distraction from the heart of the story, but rather the reverse is true – we see the glory of God in Christ breaking into the folly and the comedy of human existence. When God came down to earth, he came first to the poor and the unsophisticated, to those who were nothing in the world's scale of value. It was a group of shepherds, awkward, humorous, badly-dressed, their faces red from living rough, smelling of sheep, who were the first to kneel and worship the Saviour of the world. They would never know why God had chosen them, nor would they be very good at explaining the experience to sceptical friends and neighbours, but they have been remembered down the years in one of the most beautiful paradoxes of the Christian faith.*

SHENKYN *and* LEWIN *should be dressed in the coarse clothes of any shepherd one might see on the hills of Cumbria or Wales.* LEWIN *has a bluff exterior which disguises a nevertheless affectionate relationship with his shepherd boy. Their first words are a reference to an ancient Cumbrian sheep count.*

(GABRIEL *enters in resplendent robes. He is an awesome presence, though his manner with the audience is kindly and faintly conspiratorial as he prepares them for the entrance of the shepherds*)

GABRIEL: Pay attention.
My name is Gabriel,
I stand in the presence of God
Higher than all angels
Except Michael.
Are you ready?
(*He gestures to the stage around him*)
The fields outside Bethlehem. Two shepherds are looking for their sheep. (*We hear the sound of bleating and the distant cries of the shepherds*) Wait here. I'm going to tell them about the child that is to be born to Mary and Joseph. (*He steps aside and stands motionless.* SHENKYN *rushes on, out of breath*)

SHENKYN: (*He looks around wildly and begins to count sheep in the direction of the audience*) Wuntherum, twotherum, cockerum, cutherum (*pronounced 'queue-therum'*), shetherum, shatherum, wineberry, wigtail . . . tarry diddle? Den? (*He sighs*) I've lost two sheep. (*He cheers up on seeing* GABRIEL) Excuse me, sir. Can you advise me? (*He is puzzled that* GABRIEL *makes no response; not even looking at him*) Parlez-vous anglais? (*Silence*) Sprechen Sie Deutsch? (*He starts to inspect this strange 'statue' more closely, unaware that* LEWIN *has entered behind him*)

LEWIN: Wuntherum, twotherum, cockerum, cutherum, shetherum, shatherum, wineberry, wigtail . . . tarry diddle?

Den? Two of our best sheep. (*Calling the boy who is hidden behind* GABRIEL) *Shenkyn!* (SHENKYN *appears*) You nutcase! Leave you alone for half an hour and – chaos! Sheep jumping off the cliff, rushing into the woods, hiding in little holes.

SHENKYN: It always happens to me, sir.

LEWIN: Perhaps it's the look of your face, boy. Sheep are very choosy animals.

SHENKYN: Well, you can't blame me for that.

LEWIN: I can't blame the sheep, either. Wait, I'll ask this gentleman if he's seen two sheep. (*Going over to* GABRIEL) Excuse me, sir, have you seen two sheep? (GABRIEL *remains unmoved, staring out into the audience*) Hello, hello?

SHENKYN: (*Helpfully*) I think he's foreign, Mr Lewin.

LEWIN: Yes, well, I've handled this sort of situation before. (*He steps back a few paces and addresses* GABRIEL *in the absurdly loud tones of the British tourist abroad*) HALLO! (*Changing to a French accent*) Allo! Bon. (*Moving closer and reverting to English*) Two. Yes? Sheep. SHEEP. Yes. Gone. Perdu. Kaput. No . . . idea? No. (*With sudden inspiration he attempts a sheep impression*) Hop, hop, baaaa. Good. Two hop, hop baaaas have, er, hopped it. (*He chuckles momentarily at his own joke, then gives up in disgust*) You have a go.

SHENKYN: (*Trying to catch* GABRIEL's *eye*) Excuse me, sir, we were wondering . . . Mr Lewin?

LEWIN: Yes?

SHENKYN: There's a strange glow on this man's face.

LEWIN: Don't worry about that. They've probably all got it where he comes from. Go on.

SHENKYN: Excuse me, sir, but we've lost two-wooo! (GABRIEL *moves for the first time, gesturing towards the sky.* SHENKYN *follows his arm*) M-M-Mr Lewin! (*He rushes back to* LEWIN) There's not just one of him now, there's a whole lot more!

LEWIN: I expect they're here on holiday. Now, go on.

SHENKYN: (*Turning nervously to look up at the sky*) Er, anyway, we . . . Mr Lewin.

LEWIN: Yes, what is it?

SHENKYN: (*Controlling a rising sense of panic*) There must be about five thousand of them by now and their eyes are red like fire and their hair as white as driven SNOW! MR LEWIN! (*He jumps into* LEWIN*'s arms. They slowly disentangle themselves*)

LEWIN: (*With a calmness he does not feel*) Don't panic, boy. Try and speak to them.

SHENKYN: (*Hesitatingly he approaches the heavenly host*) Hello – everybody. Oh, Mr Lewin, there are thousands upon thousands cascading from heaven, laughing and singing, with six wings, with eight wings, some small as your little finger, others a hundred feet tall. Angels, sir, angels!

LEWIN: It's not normal.

SHENKYN: No, sir, it's most unusual. I can see a door in heaven opened and from this door come thousands upon thousands of

people in great splendour. There are
horsemen and chariots circling the
moon. Dogs baying and every kind of
animal and people coming like the
waves of the sea. Oh, Mr Lewin, I'm
afraid that we've died and gone to
heaven!

LEWIN: (*As they sink to their knees in prayer*)
Oh, God, have mercy upon us.

GABRIEL: (*Who has been watching all this*) Do not
be afraid.
(*Both shepherds let out a yell of fear.
They spin round towards* GABRIEL,
*collapsing in a heap. They are transfixed
as he speaks*) For, behold, I bring you
good news of a great joy which will
come to all the people. For to you is
born this day in the city of David a
Saviour, who is Christ the Lord. And
this will be a sign for you: you will find a
babe wrapped in swaddling clothes and
lying in a manger. Glory to God in the
highest and on earth peace among men
with whom He is pleased. (*He leaves.*
LEWIN *and* SHENKYN *slowly pick
themselves up, as if awaking from a
dream*)

LEWIN: I have seen a vision.

SHENKYN: Listen – the angels are singing 'Glory to
God in the highest'.

LEWIN: (*Gazing out into the night sky*) They are
like the clouds at sunset, layer upon
layer, as each one falls back the sky
becomes more beautiful.

SHENKYN: The sound of their voices is like the
thunder of water showering into a
mighty ocean.

LEWIN: The sound of their voices is like a

waterfall of golden coins.

SHENKYN: Rivers bursting into the desert.

LEWIN: Thunder upon thunder upon thunder.

BOTH: Glory to God in the highest and on earth peace among men with whom he is pleased.

SHENKYN: (*After a pause*) Look, dirt becoming a green leaf! (*He touches the ground beside him*) A piece of dust turning into a flower.

LEWIN: This singing will change the universe into paradise.

SHENKYN: (*Getting up*) Oh, God, that you have granted this to us! Me and Mr Lewin!

LEWIN: And to think, Lord, that you have come to dwell on earth in a humble stable, when you could have had a bedroom in my house, with Annie, Jim, Dick and Peter . . .

SHENKYN: (*Interrupting him gently*) The singing has stopped now. I'll never hear anything like that again.

LEWIN: My wife isn't going to believe this. Not likely. (*Mimicking her*) Angels! Oh, yes, and do you know what time it is? Bop, bop. (*He cowers from an imaginary rolling-pin*) Angels!

SHENKYN: How do you explain them, Mr Lewin?

LEWIN: You don't explain them, Shenkyn, you can't – I mean: 'Sorry I'm late, my dear, but we've just seen about three million angels singing hallelujah, peace on earth and goodwill to everybody down here.'

SHENKYN: You can't really, can you?

LEWIN: We'll have to break it to them gently, piece by piece, it's a very shocking thing, truth.

SHENKYN: Oh.

LEWIN: Yes. What with the present state of affairs, it's a rare commodity and very upsetting when it happens. Upsets the routine. Puts it right out of action.

SHENKYN: It can mean that you miss supper altogether. Well, what are we going to say?

LEWIN: We'll say . . . 'There was this stable' – No, we'll . . . we'll get to the door and say, 'My goodness me, just look at the time!' No. No, we'll say, 'A funny thing happened to me on the way –' No.

SHENKYN: But you know what the missus will say, anyway.

LEWIN: I do. But I won't let her. I'll say my bit. It's not every day that God gives you an excuse to be late like this. I'll say to her quite simply and she'll understand, 'All these angels came along to tell me . . . that God has come into the world and, um, I've been along to see him in this, er, small stable . . .'

SHENKYN: And you know what she'll say?

LEWIN: I've a feeling I do.

SHENKYN: She'll say . . .

LEWIN: God in a stable?

SHENKYN: Flippin' fable!

BOTH: And get your feet down off the table!

LEWIN: Come on. (*They go off to Bethlehem singing the first few lines of* 'Good Christian Men Rejoice')

Stable Talk

JOSEPH

From our earliest childhood, all of us have experienced those 'magical' moments on Christmas Eve, at night with snow falling outside. Firelight, carols and fairy lights can sometimes conjure feelings which are no more than sentimental but, for Christians who are genuinely celebrating the birth of Christ, that special sense of expectation on Christmas Eve can be touched, here and there, with awe and wonder. This is a sketch to echo that mood. What are a father's feelings at the birth of a child? Especially a father like Joseph, who had such a minor role in the whole event?

Monologues are difficult to perform; they require great concentration from both actor and audience. But this one may be useful to a group with limited resources or limited space or even to someone giving a talk or taking a Christmas service in, say, a hospital ward. The secret is not so much learning the lines as creating the character. Here, JOSEPH is portrayed as the master carpenter – rough clothes, placid temperament, a twinkle in his eye, a man who can talk easily about God without sounding pious and who takes great satisfaction from any job done well. His attitude to the new-born child is very matter-of-fact. Maybe he speaks in a West Country accent?

JOSEPH *is sitting, holding the baby. He talks to it seriously.*

> What a world to come into, eh? Hustle and bustle. Everybody travelling away from home, filling in forms, being pushed around. People shouting. And how do you like it, after four hours or

so? Mmm? (*Pause*) Your mother's asleep and those nice shepherds have gone home and if you could open your eyes, I'd show you a lovely star, wouldn't I? (*He gets up and stands looking upwards*) Through the holes in the roof. (*He chuckles*) What a fine time to come, eh? I had a feeling you were going to do this to us. And we had a nice room all ready for you back home, see? I made you a little bed. Proper little bed, all planed smooth with no nasty splinters. I set it on rockers and carved a little lamb into the headboard. You'll see it when we get back to Nazareth. You'll like it. Well, I hope so, because I wouldn't like you to think your father wanted you to be born in this old feeding trough. (*Carefully, he puts the child back in the crib*) One of the legs is a bit wobbly. Well, that's nails, you see. Never trust nails. That should have been jointed, good and proper. Takes a little care, that's all. And now I've got to take care of you as well. (*Peering solemnly at the sleeping baby*) I know who you are, you see. You don't know who I am, though, do you? (*He sighs*) I've not really had anything to do with you. (*He sits and then begins again, as if introducing a new topic of conversation*) I wish I was your father – you're so beautiful. But I'm just standing in, as you might say, for someone else. Well, at least you won't have people saying, 'Oh look, he's got his father's nose!' That's something to be grateful for. But do you know what I think? (*He takes a*

deep breath) I think you are going to
have your real father's temperament.
Because, you see, your father is a
loving, kind, mighty, glorious,
everlasting God. (*Pause*) And – (*He
leans over confidentially*) the angel
in my dream told me that you are
going to save your people from their
sins . . . which does seem a lot to ask of
a little chap like you. But I think I shall
be pretty proud of you anyway. You're
still part of my family, you see. And it's
a good family. Oh, yes. We go back a
long way. I may only be a carpenter, but
your great, great, great, great, great,
great grandfather was King. There. He
was. King David. (*Musing to himself*)
We've had kings, priests, farmers,
carpenters and now we've got a king
again . . . I think I'm a little bit chuffed
about that. (*He gets up and strolls
around*) In fact, I'm really delighted.
I'm so happy, I might even sing you a
song in a minute but you might cry, so
perhaps I'd better keep quiet. You just
carry on sleeping – I'll keep an eye on
that star and make sure nothing
happens to you as long as I'm alive.

The God Slot

CHAIRMAN; HILARY SCOTT, *a television producer;* JIM, *a novice broadcaster*

This sketch was originally broadcast in the comedy film 'WARP', made for Central Television and featuring members of the Riding Lights Theatre Company. 'WARP' (Worldwide Anglican Renewal Project) was an imaginary centre, where bishops could send their clergymen on training courses to 'face up to the twentieth century'. Therapy was on offer for anyone showing tendencies towards orthodox Christianity. A variety of refresher courses was on the curriculum, including one on the techniques of religious broadcasting. JIM was portrayed as a benign clergyman (he could be a lay person) experiencing his first training session under HILARY SCOTT, an extrovert and domineering TV producer. Although the original was set in a television studio with cameras and lights, for theatrical purposes it can be treated as a mock-up, the only prop necessary being a chair. The best way of involving the audience is to treat them all as conference members, and to pre-arrange a few people to carry scripts, which HILARY can collect during her demonstration.

Enter CHAIRMAN, *followed by* HILARY SCOTT. *He steps forward to address the audience.*

> CHAIRMAN: May I welcome you all to 'Medium with a Message', our conference on religious broadcasting? Over the next few days, various experts will be giving a course of lectures ranging from how to make simple truths look complex, how to turn Christianity into a sentimental singsong

on Sundays, and finally how to work out your personal grievances towards God on Channel Four. Our first guest is Hilary Scott, who has worked on pretty well every religious programme: *Stars on Sunday*, *Songs of Praise*, *Encounter*, *Everyman*, *The Rock Gospel Show*, *Credo*, *Highway*, party political broadcasts – in fact, there's very little that she doesn't know about religion and television. (*Turning to* HILARY) Hilary, welcome.

HILARY: Thank you, Donald. It's lovely to be here.

CHAIRMAN: Now I know you only have a few minutes before rushing back to the studio in London, for tonight's edition of *Doubt and Dogma*, so what advice would you offer to beginners in religious broadcasting?

HILARY: Well, Donald, I prefer not to offer advice. I like to demonstrate. Television is about pictures. About seeing for *ourselves*, and so I'd like to demonstrate a few techniques.

CHAIRMAN: That sounds marvellous.

HILARY: Some of us have been working very hard this afternoon, in a workshop on religious epilogues, and what I'm going to do now is collect a few of the scripts and then commandeer a volunteer.

CHAIRMAN: (*Taking his position in the audience*) Over to you, then.

HILARY: (*Breezily*) Right, have we all done our little bit? (*Various members of the audience hold up their scripts, which she collects*) 'Facing up to Bereavement'. Keith. Good. 'Coping with an Elderly

Relative'. Susan. That's marvellous.
'The Crisis of Confidence in Western
Democracy and the Critical Function of
Neo-Marxist Praxis in the Context of
Liberation Theology in Ecuador.' Not
really suitable for pensioners in
Whitstable, is it, Colin? I did say 'the
average viewer', not the top six
members of Mensa. Right? Jim, 'The
Message of Christmas'. Super. And
Barbara, 'Why Will No One Listen to
Me?'
(HILARY *leafs through forty
closely-handwritten pages*) Yes . . .
Okay, would anyone except Barbara
like to volunteer? (JIM *puts his hand up*)
Jim. 'The Message of Christmas.'
Wonderful. (*She beckons* JIM *up to the
front and sits him on the chair*) Well
done, Jim, it takes a lot of courage,
even in a training session. Now, I've
said it lots and lots of times, but I shall
say it again, and I shall keep saying it,
'Try to forget the cameras.' (*Turning to
the audience*) Okay, everyone? Jim, you
look marvellous. Lean back, relax,
darling. You're at home. Speaking to
someone else in their home. And *cue*!

JIM: Hello. Christmas is full of wonderful
        things. Carols by candlelight, turkeys,
        presents, stockings –

HILARY: Hold it. You can cut all that out, Jim.
        It's waffle. It's padding. Get to the
        point. We've only got five minutes.

JIM: Yes, right, er . . . Hello. Have you ever
        wondered what it would be like to meet
        an angel?

HILARY: Relevance, darling. Keep it relevant

and simple and inside the experience of
the viewer.

JIM: Right, er . . . There was this . . .
person, who went up to the Virgin Mary
and –

HILARY: I don't think we want to stir up a
hornets' nest of problems in our little
five minutes' broadcast, do we?
Remember, our aim is to simplify, to
reach the lowest common denominator,
and then go below it. All right? And
cue!

JIM: And the person said to the young girl,
he shall be called Jesus and shall be a
light to all people.

HILARY: Jim, darling. I really have got to stop
you again. Now, *think* about it.

JIM: What?

HILARY: 'A light to *all* people?' Was that very
sensitive to our minority groups? Try to
think of something that would be of
equal appeal to a young white mother of
two, a Rastafarian, a Jewish rabbi, a
middle-aged couple in Hornsea and a
78-year-old Iranian member of the
Ba'hai faith. All right? Good. (*Turning
to the audience*) A round of applause for
a marvellous guinea-pig. (JIM *looks
round, puzzled, then – realising this
refers to him – shuffles back to his seat in
the audience. The* CHAIRMAN *joins*
HILARY.)

CHAIRMAN: Well, it's easy to see why Hilary has had
such a successful career in religious
television. (*Turning to her*) Have you
any final comment for us tonight?

HILARY: Yes. The important thing is to
communicate. People come to me

burning with a message, but no way of communicating it. Television reverses that process. It gives them a burning desire to communicate, but absolutely nothing to say. This is easily the best way to avoid offence and keep religious programmes on the air.

CHAIRMAN: Hilary Scott, thank you very much. (*He leads the audience in applause, then escorts her offstage*)

Getting Ready

WOMAN; MAN; TEENAGE BOY; VICAR; CHORUS; VOICE

Preparations for Christmas start earlier and earlier these days as the commercial machine starts winding itself up from mid October. By the final week before the great day the pressure is enormous, frantic and obsessive: 'Did they send us a card last year? Whom have we forgotten? Where will everybody sleep? I've run out of icing sugar. I don't care whether she's a vegetarian, I'm not cooking two dinners! What on earth can we get Daddy on our pocket money?' Late on Christmas Day most of us collapse from a mixture of food and nervous exhaustion. Almost proverbially, the baby Jesus is excluded in the whirlwind of activity. But what if the risen Christ in all his glory were forgotten, too? Now read on.

Wherever 'rhythm' is indicated, the four characters make up a human clock. If a larger choral group is possible, they create the clock behind the action and sustain the rhythm throughout the sketch, keeping the sound low through the spoken passages and high through the rhythm sections. The sound can be more sophisticated than the simple 'Tick-Tock' suggested here – a grandfather clock with a whirring chain and pendulum might be effective. When only the four characters are used, they re-form the clock between the dialogue. This can be worked out through improvisation. One solution is for the VICAR to represent the minute hands, starting at ten minutes to midnight; the MAN and the WOMAN to use their right and left arms respectively to create the continuous circle of the second hand as it ticks round. The sketch begins with the rhythm of the clock.

RHYTHM: TICK-TOCK, TICK-TOCK, TICK-TOCK, TICK-TOCK.

ALL: It's Christmas Eve, it's Christmas Eve
And time is running out, is running out,
is running out.

RHYTHM: TICK-TOCK, TICK-TOCK,
TICK-TOCK, TICK-TOCK.

WOMAN: The pudding!

MAN: The presents!

BOY: The fairy lights!

VICAR: The sermon!

RHYTHM: TICK-TOCK, TICK-TOCK,
TICK-TOCK, TICK-TOCK.

WOMAN: This year everything is going to be
under control. My mother-in-law is *not*
coming into the kitchen and there's
going to be no nonsense over Camilla
saying she's gone vegetarian! The dog is
not going to sit in the cranberry jelly
and dinner will begin well before the six
o'clock news! If only I had time!

MAN: This year *I'm* looking after the
Sellotape! There will be no arguments
about the nauseating pink of the
wrapping paper and every present will
be clearly labelled and round the tree by
midnight, not halfway through the
Queen's speech! And this year Kevin
will not be given a 'Changing the Guard'
tin drum in his stocking! If only I had
time!

BOY: This year the fairy lights are going to
work! They are not going to flash on and
off and then fuse for the whole of
Christmas Day! Every bulb will be
checked and wired up in sequence.
We're not going to have the Royal
Ballet on all afternoon, either! All the
important programmes will be clearly
marked with a red pen in the *TV Times*!

If only I had time!

VICAR: This year I am going to preach a meaningful Christmas sermon! I will not have Darth Vader or a cuddly Care Bear in the pulpit, nor will I ruin my sermon notes with one of those dolls that wets themselves! I will think through everything beforehand and preach on the relevance of the birth of Christ to the modern world! If only I had time!

RHYTHM: TICK-TOCK, TICK-TOCK, TICK-TOCK, TICK-TOCK.

WOMAN: So much to do!

MAN: So much to wrap!

BOY: So much to fix!

VICAR: So much to say!

ALL: If only I had time!

RHYTHM: TICK-TOCK, TICK-TOCK, TICK-TOCK, TICK-TOCK.

(*The four characters increase their flurry of activity*)

WOMAN: Where's the stuffing?

MAN: Who's got the scissors?

BOY: Who's got the screwdriver?

VICAR: Where's that handbook to the Bible?

WOMAN: If only those carol singers hadn't scoffed all the mince pies!

MAN: Who bought this revolting pink paper?

BOY: Who trod on the fairy?

VICAR: My mind's a blank! I should never have had that sherry!

RHYTHM: TICK-TOCK, TICK-TOCK, TICK-TOCK, TICK-TOCK.

ALL: Hurry up, it's nearly Christmas!

WOMAN: I need a microwave!

MAN: I need the scissors!

BOY: I need a fuse!

VICAR: I need another sherry!

WOMAN: So much to finish!

MAN: So much to organise!

BOY: So much to mend!

VICAR: So little to say!

RHYTHM: TICK-TOCK, TICK-TOCK,
TICK-TOCK, TICK-TOCK,
TICK-TOCK, TICK-TOCK,
TICK-TOCK, TICK-TOCK.

ALL: Two minutes to go!

RHYTHM: TICK-TOCK, TICK-TOCK, TICK-
(*The rhythm stops abruptly. The clock is silent. The activity ceases*)

WOMAN: That's strange. The oven timer's gone off.

MAN: My watch has stopped.

BOY: The video's flashing.

VICAR: Why is everything so quiet?
(*Slowly they look around*)
It's daylight outside . . .

MAN: The whole sky is on fire!

WOMAN: The light is blinding!

BOY: What on earth – (*He freezes*)

WOMAN: What's happeni – (*She freezes*)

MAN: This is extraor – (*He freezes*)

VICAR: Impossi – (*He freezes*)

VOICE: (*Off*) The Son of Man comes at an hour you do not expect.

Note. This sketch has an obvious connection with the final section of the book, 'Advent (The Second Coming)', but we have included it here to emphasise the irony that Christmas is the time of year when the return of Christ is perhaps least expected.

NEW YEAR'S DAY

New Year celebrations are a hangover (literally for most people) from pagan festivals. They have little to do with the Christian religion, with the exception of the watchnight service on New Year's Eve, which is a comparatively recent attempt to add a little sanctity to the occasion. For many, celebrating New Year means going to parties, getting drunk, behaving in an embarrassing fashion with someone else's wife and then joining hands with a total stranger and singing 'Till auld acquaintance be forgot'. For others, it means staying at home and blasting the mind with violent movies on television. An anthropologist from Mars would certainly regard it as a very curious custom; he might well conclude that the last thing we want to do is celebrate the future year – we merely want to forget the last one.

The Church has never quite known what to do about New Year festivities. As early as AD 567, the Second Council of Tours refers to the need for special fasts and Masses of expiation on New Year's Day as a direct re-action to the excesses of the Roman Saturnalia, a season of wild merriment that still survived. Different dates for the New Year throughout the Christian era (Christmas Day, Lady Day, Easter Day, March 1st and March 25th have all been regarded as New Year's Day in the past), with the choice finally landing on a day of no great liturgical signi-ficance (the Feast of the Circumcision), have meant that the celebration of New Year's Day frequently lacks the re-ligious significance that it demands. The Hebrew Feast of New Year, for instance, tempers the mood of joy and celebration with a sense of accountability to God and the need for penitence. Blessing for the New Year is linked to forgiveness for the old.

Naturally, the modern Christian should never be a killjoy

at New Year, but his joy must take a deeper root than any superficial entertainment can provide. The urgency of facing the moral challenge of New Year is something that society as a whole needs to recognise, as well as the individual. In the twentieth century, we can never be sure that there will be a New Year. For this reason, we have picked up the obvious moral element in New Year traditions – the making of resolutions – and written a satirical sketch. The tone of the sketch makes it suitable for revue programmes or youth evenings, rather than the normal church service: its performance will depend on the mood of an occasion (and it can be performed throughout the Christmas season, or at any other time in the year when there is a need for a sharp reminder of human selfishness).

A Prosperous New Year

FOUR ACTORS, *of either sex, self-consciously living up to the sharp and aggressive image projected by performers in tabloid newspaper commercials.*

This sketch is a darkly ironic send-up of 'hard-sell' television advertising. It satirises the values and preoccupations of our society in a style which is deliberately distasteful. By twisting various common New Year resolutions, and making them sound highly desirable, the sketch boldly proclaims a quick route to successful selfishness. The lines of doggerel which encapsulate each resolution could well be set to music to increase the overall impression of hollow slickness, while the whole piece would benefit from a pulsating accompaniment. We leave this to your imaginations. Punchy delivery, at times brash, at times silky smooth, is of the essence; where possible, this can be enhanced by individual spotlighting. The actors make fast entrances and then assume various poses before delivering their lines.

ONE: (*Brandishing a copy of the newspaper*)
Ring in the New Year with *The Scum*!
Amazing! Sensational! Controversial!
The Scum! Don't miss this fantastic
fifty-page edition, exclusively for you!
All you need to know about sport,
television, girls, fashion, crime, girls,
sex and girls. It's all *new* in *The Scum*!
Plus a full-colour, ten-page pull-out:
how to kick that habit and keep those
New Year resolutions rolling; one
hundred rock-solid resolutions
exclusively for YOU! Resolutions on a
host of your favourite subjects. Here's
just a few.

TWO: RESOLUTION NUMBER ONE.

THREE: Be nicer to other people . . . whenever it is directly to your advantage. Don't waste valuable time making friends with those less influential than yourself. Learn how to forget a face and ignore the plain and dull at parties!

TOGETHER: *Cut through the dross, make friends with the boss.*

ONE: RESOLUTION NUMBER TWO.

FOUR: Give up smoking. Take up burning . . . with lust! Stop thinking constantly of making it with your secretary and *make it* with your secretary!

TOGETHER: *Don't sit there and vex, get on with the sex.*

THREE: RESOLUTION NUMBER THREE.

TWO: Discipline your mind. Fill your head with trivia! Turn off those heavy TV programmes. Turn on those light, light comedies.

TOGETHER: *Have a ball, don't think at all.*

FOUR: RESOLUTION NUMBER FOUR.

ONE: Let's have a year of driving without convictions . . . scruples, morals or principles! Be considerate on the roads. Use the whole width. And drivers, think before you drink . . . have I got enough brown paperbags in the car?

TOGETHER: *Be thoroughly crass, just step on the gas.*

TWO: RESOLUTION NUMBER FIVE.

THREE: Be more helpful to your friends. Don't keep them in the dark, share your gossip immediately!

TOGETHER: *Lying's okay, spread a rumour today.*

ONE: RESOLUTION NUMBER SIX.

FOUR: Keep up an irresponsible attitude to the needs of others and thus save money!

Become like your dog . . . fat and
dozing by the fire.

TOGETHER: *Why help a child in need, when Fido*
wants a feed?

THREE: RESOLUTION NUMBER SEVEN.

TWO: Cut out those little twinges of
conscience. Don't think about religion!
Obliterate all moments of reflection
after bad news and funerals. Just turn
on those light, light comedies!

TOGETHER: *Never admit to any fears, go lightly*
dancing through the years.

ONE: PLUS!

FOUR: How to be more punctual . . . in
satisfying your own desires.

THREE: How to turn over a new leaf . . . and see
the girl on Page three.

TWO: How to keep your SOUL under
CONTROL!

ONE: All this and much, much more valuable
advice in *The Scum* – Britain's number
one paper!

THREE: Britain prefers *The Scum*!

TWO: Make those resolutions with *The Scum*!

FOUR: Make 19— the International Year of –

TOGETHER: YOURSELF!

EPIPHANY

'Behold, wise men from the East came to Jerusalem, saying, "Where is he who was born king of the Jews? For we have seen his star in the East, and have come to worship him."'

The story of the wise men has haunted the imagination of artists, writers, theologians, and generations of children, for this is one of the most mysterious and awe-inspiring episodes in the Bible. Rubens and Rembrandt painted pictures, T. S. Eliot wrote a famous poem, scientists and astronomers argue about the star, but no one knows who these men were, nor even how many there were, nor where they came from. As for the star, which travelled across the sky to 'rest over the place' where Jesus was, we shall probably never know its identity. The feast of the Epiphany, as it is celebrated in the Western Church, commemorates this remarkable pilgrimage.

Epiphany (meaning a manifestation of divine power) celebrates other events, such as the Nativity, the Baptism of Christ, and the Wedding at Cana, all revealing the nature of Jesus as Son of God, but the festival is most closely linked with the revelation of God's power to the Gentiles. These ancient philosophers had come seeking no ordinary being. Aided by the knowledge of their civilisation, they had come seeking a greater knowledge. If they were men of power and influence, which their gifts suggest, they had come to pay tribute to one of greater power and influence. At the Epiphany of God, in Christ, we are told that they 'rejoiced exceedingly with great joy'. Their quest had been fulfilled, and they fell down and worshipped a tiny baby. This is one of the most moving paradoxes in the story of Christ coming into the world: even as a helpless child, he commanded authority over the wisdom of the world.

This is a key to our celebration of the festival. The twentieth century is no different from the first, in that wisdom rarely bows to the revelation of Christ. When it does, it produces a new kind of wisdom, one that is touched with humility and with the infinitely greater wisdom of God himself. We may suppose that the wise men returned with this gift of divine wisdom, in return for theirs of gold, frankincense and myrrh. However, for the most part, intellectual pride and – perhaps even worse – a preference for false wisdom, prevents that act of submission to the truth.

We have taken the rise of astrology in the twentieth century as a relevant example of such a substitute wisdom; for the nature of the wise men's study of the stars quite clearly led them to a different conclusion from any fortune-teller or quack star-gazer of today. The wise men, no doubt, would have a great deal to say to some people today who are intent on making fortunes out of pretending to tell them.

The sketch is directed to an adult audience, not least because the journey of the wise men is frequently drama-tised as a children's story (and groups can produce their own material here). The tone is satirical, but the purpose is very serious, for there are few more urgent issues than the quest for true wisdom in a world of dangerous counter-feits.

Wise Men from the West

READER OF THE LESSON; DOREEN PAPP *and* KEVIN MOZARELLA, *astrologers*

This sketch begins with a reading from an imaginary book of the Bible, commenting on the folly of some of our practices in the West. If performed during a service of worship, it is essential that it is quite clearly announced as a sketch before the 'reading' takes place, to avoid any unnecessary shock to the congregation, who (if not prepared) might take offence at the parody. Needless to say, this little monologue that prefaces the main sketch can be treated as a one-minute cameo performance on its own. The main sketch that follows should be staged like a radio or TV Breakfast Show, *with the resident astrologers making their predictions to microphones, or unseen cameras, and a studio audience. They are self-consciously 'show-biz', with extravagant clothes –* DOREEN, *heavily made-up, with huge glasses and dangly earrings,* KEVIN *with a loud suit and rather dinky little shoes, somewhat camp and OTT. However, actors should beware of overacting parts like these. Extroversion of this kind needs some subtlety of interpretation, otherwise it can become irritating to the audience and the performance may stand in the way of the material.*

KEVIN *and* DOREEN *should not take their seats until the reading is over. The* READER *should be in Sunday best, treating his or her task with dignity. Good timing is needed, but the manner should follow traditional church readings as closely as possible, straight-faced, avoiding any awareness of the comedy.*

The READER *approaches the lectern, turns over the pages of the 'Bible' solemnly, and reads.*

READER: Now it came to pass in those days that
certain wise men arose in the West,
saying, 'Behold, we have seen the stars,
even as it has been foretold, and verily,
Tuesday will be a lucky day for
Sagittarians.' And the people marvelled
greatly, and were exceedingly
impressed, and in like manner they too
consulted the stars and did come up
with a load of rubbish, yea verily, a pack
of lies, so that the primitive tribes of the
earth murmured among themselves,
saying, 'If this is where Western
civilisation has got the human race, you
can keep it, mate.' Notwithstanding, a
great multitude of the western press,
and other mighty organs of the media,
did daily publish abroad the sayings of
the astrologers, so much so that the wise
men from the East were all but
forgotten, and the Star of Bethlehem
became only a dim memory, and the
crying of a child in a manger was
drowned by the clink of money, crossing
the palms of the false prophets. And in
those days a deep darkness fell upon
the face of the land.

The READER *closes the 'Bible' and returns
to his seat. Ideally, a jingle (live or
recorded) should introduce* DOREEN *and*
KEVIN, *with a voice-over: 'Ladies and
gentlemen, will you please welcome
Kevin Mozarella and Doreen Papp.'
Canned applause.*

KEVIN: Thank you and welcome to another
edition of 'Star Turns', Britain's number

one programme for predictions. Well, Doreen, what do you think of the remarkable zones of astral energy in the Milky Way this morning?

DOREEN: Astonishing, Kevin. A magical mix of the sun, the new moon and Mercury, with Mars parallel to Pluto, Venus conjoined to Saturn, and the electric vibes of Jupiter throbbing across the asteroid belt.

KEVIN: Any thoughts about a general forecast for the future?

DOREEN: Well, first of all, I think we can safely assume that all star signs will experience a number of features in common.

KEVIN: Such as?

DOREEN: Most people will either receive an unexpected caller, make an important decision and have an upsurge of romantic feelings, or experience none of these things at all.

KEVIN: Can we take this as a likely prediction?

DOREEN: Oh, I think so, Kevin. Most people will also spend a few minutes every day in a small room, apart from others, and this will be a significant time, depending on the reading matter available. In addition to this, over three million people will not face important business decisions in the coming year, and the fourteenth, seventeenth and twentieth days of the month will be lucky days for those who are employed, as will every other day.

KEVIN: Now it's time for our 'Alternative Sources of Information Spot', and it's back to you, Doreen, to tell us a little bit about the ancient art of divining the future from the entrails of animals.

DOREEN: Thank you, Kevin. Well, I've been taking a quick look at some chicken livers, sheeps' intestines and rabbit droppings (*She produces a nasty looking bag, probably not transparent*) and I think it would be fair to say that these have a lot more to say about the future than the average religious programme on television.

KEVIN: (*Peering into the bag*) I'm intrigued by those chicken livers, Doreen.

DOREEN: So was I. In fact, they made a nasty mess on the kitchen floor this morning when I threw them over my shoulder, and this usually means that there are problems ahead, especially for the chickens.

KEVIN: Finally, a letter from Mr K. Herod of Jerusalem. (*Reading*) 'Dear Kevin, I am worried about my future. Some men with silly hats on and funny accents came round the other day, and asked to see the King of the Jews. I thought it was a practical joke and I laughed heartily. However, it soon became clear that they did not know I was the King of the Jews and, worse than that, they insisted they were looking for a little baby. At this, I stamped my feet and screamed for my mother, but this did not convince them, and they went off to Bethlehem. Since then, things have been very quiet in Jerusalem, and the worship has fallen off considerably. What should I do? Yours sincerely, K. Herod.' Well, Mr Herod, if I am right in thinking that you are a Libran, the best thing is to believe in yourself. Have confidence. If you are the King of the Jews, don't shout about it, just be what you are. As for these rumours, I think the best thing is to stifle them wherever possible. (*Turning to Doreen*) What do you think?

DOREEN: I agree with Kevin, here. There is always someone who comes along and tells you that you've got it all wrong. Have confidence in yourself, your own philosophy, your own destiny. Don't bother with ridiculous superstitions.

KEVIN: So squash those doubts and fears thoroughly, Mr Herod. Kill off every suspicion that you may be wrong. That's all we have time for, toni – oh! (*Turning over the letter*) There's a P.S. here. 'Do you know anything about the star over Bethlehem?' (*Shrugging his shoulders and looking at Doreen, who shakes her head*) We haven't heard of that at all, and it certainly doesn't appear in our charts, but I shouldn't worry. It's probably a bit of grit on your telescope. That's all from 'Star Turns', so from Doreen and myself, goodnight.

DOREEN: Goodnight.

(*Repeat jingle, with canned applause, as they leave.*)

The sketch can then be followed by a genuine reading from the Bible. The best, in this context, is Romans 1:18–22 (RSV).

'For the wrath of God is revealed from heaven against all ungodliness and wickedness of men who by their wickedness suppress the truth. For what can be known about God is plain to them, because God has shown it to them. Ever since the creation of the world his invisible nature, namely, his eternal power and deity, has been clearly perceived in the things that have been made. So they are without excuse; for although they knew God they did not honour him as God or give thanks to him, but they became futile in their thinking and their senseless minds were darkened. Claiming to be wise, they became fools . . .'

WEEK OF PRAYER FOR CHRISTIAN UNITY

The scandal of disunity among Christians and the urgent need for united prayer and witness to the world should concern all those who seek to follow Christ. In recent years, this has been the focus of 'The Week of Prayer for Christian Unity', which was first introduced by a group of Anglicans in 1938. Since then it has grown into an international event promoted by both the World Council of Churches and the Vatican Secretariat for Promoting Christian Unity. The first observance of the 'Christian Unity Octave' (a period of eight days) by Anglicans and Roman Catholics was in 1908. Subsequently, in 1935, the French Abbé, Paul Couturier, launched a 'Universal Week of Prayer for Christian Unity' to pray 'for the unity Christ wills by the means he wills'.

Today, a full-colour leaflet is produced (distributed in Britain by the British Council of Churches) to promote the week. It contains a liturgy for a service of reconciliation and an eight-day sequence of readings and prayers to help Christians meditate upon their shared faith and ask God for the courage to fight together against unbelief. It is a call for a united witness amid the distress of the world. In 1986, this liturgy was prepared by an ecumenical group from Yugoslavia made up of Roman Catholic, Lutheran, Orthodox and Pentecostal churches. It opens with the words:

Greetings in the name of our Saviour Jesus Christ. We have gathered together in his name to honour God. Enlightened by the Holy Spirit we have come to pray for the unity of all Christians and the strength to witness together.

It is our hope that the little sketch offered here may amusingly highlight some of the issues and further the cause of unity wherever it may be performed.

One Faith, One Lord

THREE CHRISTIANS

To the uninitiated observer the Christian Church must seem very puzzling. Over the centuries, Christians have often stressed their differences, yet they all claim to be followers of Christ. What is the outsider to think? Will he really have the patience to discover the distinctions between a Methodist and a Baptist, a Free Churchman and a Plymouth Brother, a charismatic Anglican and a renewed Presbyterian, 'high' and Roman Catholic? To him, the Church must look very similar to the Football League: everybody is basically following the same game, while fanatically supporting different players, in different colours, some teams with a reputation for fancy footwork and attacking flair, others for simply thumping the ball into the goalmouth. A cursory glance shows the Church to be more divided than united. The Bible teaches that love never insists on its own way, so perhaps a sketch such as this, which makes fun of some of these differences, can put them in perspective and show how cosmetic they really are. Taste in worship is one thing, faith in our 'one Lord and Saviour, Jesus Christ' is quite another and much more important.

THREE CHRISTIANS *(they could be men or women or, preferably, a mixture) file on to the stage, solemnly humming the tune to the hymn, 'Thy hand, O God, has guided Thy flock from age to age.' They take up positions at the front. Their attitudes, clothes and mode of address to the audience tell us that they are different, though these distinctions are subtle, not cartooned. The third Christian is the most casual and has a warm, friendly, almost off-hand way of delivering the lines.*

ONE: My church is a high church.

TWO: My church is a low church.

THREE: (*Momentarily stuck for something apt*) My church is above sea-level. (*He shrugs*)

ONE: Besides the altar, we have chalices, chasubles, candles, acolytes and wafers.

TWO: Besides the Lord's Table, we have psalters, robes, lecterns, notice-boards and real bread.

THREE: Beside the piano, we have a box for the hymnbooks.

ONE: I find great meaning in ritual and ceremony.

TWO: I find great meaning in extempore prayer and exposition.

THREE: I don't know what any of them mean!

ONE: I read the Authorised King James Version. It has real beauty.

TWO: I read the Revised Standard Version. It has real authority.

THREE: I read the Good News Version. It's got real pictures.

ONE: We are rediscovering the charismatic essence of the liturgy of the Church.

TWO: We are rediscovering the principles of charismatic renewal in the life of the congregation.

THREE: I'm not sure, but I think our washing machine's charismatic.

ONE: We celebrate the Eucharist.

TWO: We share the Lord's Supper.

THREE: We never know what to call it either.

ONE: We always finish prayer with a suitable
       collect.

TWO: We always finish prayer by saying the
       grace.

THREE: We always finish prayer in time to watch
       Dallas. (*Or name of current TV
       programme*)

ONE: Next Sunday is Quinquagesima.

TWO: Next Sunday is the beginning of our
       Lent Course.

THREE: (*Obviously impressed with the others but
       cannot compete*)
       Er, next Sunday's the fourteenth, isn't
       it?

ONE: I find the lectionary a great source of
       meditation.

TWO: I find the sermons a great source of
       spiritual encouragement.

THREE: I find the pews a great source of
       backache.

ONE: Our worship is tastefully enhanced by a
       combination of Stanford, Tallis, Byrd
       and Gibbons.

TWO: Our worship is doctrinally balanced by a
       combination of Wesley, Watts and the
       Redemption Hymnal.

THREE: Our worship is definitely *ruined* by a
       combination of Mrs Lowde and Mrs
       Sharpe.

ONE: We have coffee in the narthex after
       matins.

TWO: We have bring-and-share lunches in the
       hall after service.

THREE: (*With deep loathing*) We have tea in green cups after *everything*!

ONE: The discipline of the Daily Office frees my spirit to meditate on higher things.

TWO: The length of the prayers allows me time for personal devotion.

THREE: Yeah, my mind tends to wander a bit, too.

ONE: But Christ is the Head of our Church.

TWO: Christ is the Cornerstone of our faith.

THREE: Christ is the rock on which we build.
(*They look at each other for a moment, puzzled by their unexpected agreement*)

ONE: (*Returning to the audience*) But I think *our* way of doing things is most *reverent*.

TWO: I think *our* way of doing things is truly *biblical*.

THREE: I'm sure there's a lot of prejudice in *our* church as well.

(*As each says the final line they turn away slightly. Freeze.*)

Note. We are indebted to Phil Potter for suggesting the theme of this sketch.

LENT

Lent is the forty-day period of preparation for the Easter festival. The word comes from the Old English for 'spring', and it is fitting that a traditional period of fasting and prayer should take place in the spring, for at this time of year the earth renews itself and the cycle of the seasons begins again. The Church, too, needs constant renewal and, although Lent originated in the early centuries as a period of preparation for baptism, it has come to signify a time when all Christians can turn from sin and renew their commitment to Christ. The forty days that run from Ash Wednesday to Easter Eve (Sundays are excluded) parallel the periods of fasting undertaken by Moses, Elijah and above all by Our Lord himself. During the Temptation in the Wilderness, Jesus fought and overcame the Devil. It was the launching of his attack on sin which, at the end of his earthly ministry, culminated in the great victories of Good Friday and Easter Day. Lent is therefore a time when we, too, can face up to the sin in our lives. Our prayer 'thy kingdom come' must first be achieved in our own hearts before it can take root in the world. Of course, all seasons are proper times for repentance and humility of spirit, but by emphasising the need for honesty towards ourselves and towards God, Lent can be a valuable period of self-examination before the great rejoicing of the Easter festival. We have written a sketch which looks at the hidden attitudes of the heart, based on the famous parable of the Pharisee and the Publican.

Judging from Appearances

NARRATOR; NORMAN, *middle-aged church treasurer, some-what set in his ways;* NICK, *a colourful character in charge of the church youth club*

The parables of Jesus are simple and vivid. They make a happy hunting-ground for the biblical sketchwriter but sometimes, because these stories have become so familiar, we miss their original shock impact. When Jesus first told them, they almost always contained an unexpected twist, a sting in the tail, which is there to clarify the deeper issues and explode the prejudice of the audience – a selfish son is welcomed home with open arms, a servant is condemned for being over-cautious, social rejects are the guests of honour at a magnificent banquet. The stories are unforgettable and often highly satirical. Here is a modern treatment of the parable of the Pharisee and the Publican, but who are the latter-day Pharisees? Whom does God accept? Too often we judge only from appearances.

Four chairs are arranged in two rows facing the audience. There is an aisle down the middle. NICK *is seated at the front on one side;* NORMAN *kneels in the second row on the other. The* NARRATOR *is free to move around them during the introductory speech before taking up a position downstage left where he or she will then administer the bread at communion. It is important that the two actors don't lead the audience to anticipate the twist at the end of the sketch. In the expression of their thoughts before they pray,* NORMAN *should convey a kind of tense self-righteousness, while* NICK *should communicate a simple, but thoughtful enthusiasm for what has been happening among the young people in the church. It is as they pray that their true colours are revealed.*

NARRATOR: Two men are about to take communion in their local church. Norman Fraser (*Pausing alongside him*), bursar of St Martin's College and treasurer of the church finance committee. And Nick Price, volunteer youth worker and former drug addict. Norman has been a member of the congregation for twenty-six years, during which he has introduced a stewardship scheme and battled hard to make the church heating system more cost-effective. Nick was introduced to the church four years ago by his probation officer. Since his conversion, Nick's lifestyle has changed in some respects. He is no longer involved in armed robbery and drug pushing, but his clothes and record number of tattoos are regarded with suspicion by some members of the congregation. (*Glances at* NORMAN) Listen to the thoughts that occur to these two men in that period of quiet reflection before taking communion.

NORMAN: (*Still kneeling*) I was far from happy with that guest service the other night. I felt the music and the drama were irreverent.

NICK: It's amazing what's happened to me over the last few years. Four years ago I'd have been down the pub right now.

NORMAN: And another thing, the collection was down twenty-five pounds on a normal week. I found that most disappointing. I thought it was typical of the modern attitude.

NICK: (*Surveying the congregation behind him*) It's great the way the youth club's growing. So many have joined since I took over. They can really identify with people like me.

NORMAN: (*Staring straight ahead over the back of the pew*) It's also been worrying me that I cannot identify with the leadership of this church. I haven't liked the new minister, and I have been extremely reluctant to give him my support.

NICK: (*Rising to come forward for communion. As he waits his turn, he stands, looking slightly upwards and prays:*) Lord, I really thank you that I became a Christian. I really thank you that I've conquered the past. I'm so happy that I can give my talents to you and that I can go anywhere and talk to anybody and bring the light of your gospel to all people who feel rejected. I really thank you that you don't have to be hypocritical and wear posh suits and put on posh voices to be a Christian. I really thank you that I'm not like that. Amen. (*He receives communion and then turns upstage to return to his seat by the centre aisle.* NORMAN *gets up. Before leaving his row he says a prayer.* NICK *freezes as he speaks*)

NORMAN: Lord, I'm ashamed of all my attitudes. How can you ever forgive me? (*He moves forward and stands with head bowed to receive the bread.* NICK *moves again to his seat*)

NARRATOR: (*About to hand the bread to* NORMAN) Jesus said, 'I tell you that this man, rather than the other, went home justified before God. For everyone who exalts himself will be humbled and he who humbles himself will be exalted.'

MOTHERING SUNDAY

Anybody who thinks that Mothering Sunday is an invention of the florists and the manufacturers of greeting cards can be forgiven, in view of the recent efforts to promote a 'Father's Day'. Within the next century we can expect to see anything ranging from 'Second-Cousin's Day' to 'Budgerigar Sunday'. However, Mothering Sunday does have genuine roots in English tradition, and is now a widely recognised theme for a family service.

Three centuries ago, the mid-Lent Sunday, the fourth Sunday in Lent, was set apart for apprentices and daughters in service to return home to their parents, often bearing with them a bunch of flowers as a token of their affection. A seventeenth-century writer observed in 1644, 'Every mid-Lent Sunday is a great day at Worcester, when all the children and godchildren meet with the head and chief of the family, and have a feast. They call it Mothering Day.' It is not clear how widely this custom was celebrated, and certainly by the early years of this century it had largely disappeared. Our present Mothering Sunday owes more to the labours of a certain Miss Anna Jarvis in America, who was so moved at the death of her mother in May 1909 that she vigorously campaigned for a national day to celebrate motherhood. This was clearly a brilliant idea, as no sensible politician would risk implying that he did not love his mother. Accordingly, on May 10th, 1913, the Senate and House of Representatives passed a resolution making the second Sunday in May 'Mother's Day'. During the Second World War, American servicemen stationed in Britain brought with them their celebration of 'Mother's Day' and the custom of giving cards, gifts and flowers.

Our Mothering Sunday kept its traditional Lenten date but absorbed most of the characteristics of 'Mother's Day'.

The two are now regarded as synonymous in Britain. The traditional gift of Mothering Sunday is a bunch of violets – or primroses if violets are unavailable – and in some parts of the country the old custom of baking simnel cakes on this day is still preserved. One further connection with the day is the liturgical description 'Laetare (rejoicing) Sunday': this is because of the opening words of the introit, 'Rejoice ye with Jerusalem'. The epistle for the day (Gal. 4) picks this up, by speaking of 'Jerusalem . . . which is the mother of us all'. Children can freely rejoice in the love of their mothers, as Christians may rejoice in the city of Zion and in the knowledge of being sons and daughters of God.

Our choice of a sketch for Mothering Sunday is a dramatisation of the parable of the Lost Sheep, for a family audience, with a particular emphasis on the sense of fun and rejoicing which seems appropriate to this day. It is worth noting that, although the parable is clearly associated in Luke's Gospel with the sinner who goes astray, the version in Matthew is told in the context of the love of God for children.

The Lost Sheep

NARRATOR; PHOEBE, *a capable shepherdess;* LAMBERT, *a lovable but independent young sheep;* CHORUS, *a flock of sheep, who behave like a group of rowdy fourth-formers over which the* NARRATOR *is unable to establish full control*

This is a familiar story told in an unfamiliar way by a group of actors, of which the NARRATOR *is the leader. Its effect should be highly theatrical and depends upon great energy, strong chorus interaction, discipline, amusing sound-effects and good timing in order to work properly. The* CHORUS *can be as large as you like. The important thing is that each member of the flock should create his or her own character and be prepared to react in complete harmony with the others. From time to time, individuals may be given occasional lines, but generally the* CHORUS *amplifies the story by acting in unison. They arrange themselves at different levels in a compact group on stage, leaving enough space for the action in front of them. It should be clear from their costume (perhaps pairs of woolly ears?) that they are a flock of sheep.*

This sketch was originally written for performance to children in the context of a family service, but it would also lend itself well to street-theatre. A giant cartoon approach is probably best for the creation of the lion: a huge lion-head can be made by holding up the various parts on sticks (the mane, the two eyes and the two jaws) and then choreographing movements to fit the action. 'FX' is a convenient shorthand for the creation of suitable sound-effects by the CHORUS.

NARRATOR: (*He stands in front of his 'class' of sheep and addresses the audience*) Once upon

a time there was a flock of sheep.
(*With appropriate baas and bleats, the
sheep illustrate the various types*) Big
ones . . . little ones . . . clever ones . . .
and thick ones . . . posh ones . . .
common ones . . . wild ones . . . and
woolly ones.

A SHEEP: (*Quavering voice*) Actually, I'm not
sure about the Resurrection.

NARRATOR: Some had horns : . . (*Someone makes a
silly French horn noise from the back of
the group. The* NARRATOR *glares at them*)
Give it to me.

SHEEP 1: (*Grumbling*) Ah, *sir*.

NARRATOR: Quickly. (*He confiscates 'the horn'*) But
most didn't. (*More surreptitiously, the
horn noise comes again*) In all – see me
afterwards – there were one hundred
sheep. (*He is rattled, but presses on lest
the whole situation should get completely
out of hand*) They were extremely
happy together.

CHORUS: (*Begin to sing the theme from
Beethoven's* 'Pastoral Symphony')

NARRATOR: It was a wonderful life. The insects
hummed,

CHORUS: (*The theme swells briefly with a hum*)

NARRATOR: The birds sang,

CHORUS: (*They sing a few bars loudly to 'la'*)

NARRATOR: And the bees buzzed.

CHORUS: (*They end the theme by 'buzzing' the last
few notes very fast*)

NARRATOR: All day long the sheep gambolled

CHORUS: (*Suddenly miming games of poker, etc.*)

NARRATOR: And frisked.

CHORUS: (*They frisk each other for offensive
weapons*)

NARRATOR: (*Sternly*) Look! Either we do this

seriously or we don't do it at all!

CHORUS: (*Improvise their apologies*)

NARRATOR: Now, in charge of the sheep was a very beautiful young shepherdess called (*mispronouncing her name*) Phoeeb . . . I'm sorry . . . Phoebe.

CHORUS: (*Wild yodelling of the goatherd song from the* 'Sound of Music' *as* PHOEBE *enters downstage*)

NARRATOR: Yes, thank you. We've all seen it. Many times. She had invented a very good way of getting a lot of sheep into a small space. The sheepfold. First, fold the sheep and then put them into a small space. Ha! Ha! Ha! No, really, she took great care of the sheep. (PHOEBE *mimes the various tasks with different sheep*) She loved them,

CHORUS: (*FX Sentimental Aaaaaahh*)

NARRATOR: She fed them, she watered them, she led them. She removed awkward little stones from their hooves and awkward little stains from their woollens with a regular warm wash

CHORUS: (*FX Washing machine*)

NARRATOR: And spin.

CHORUS: (*FX, Action fast spin cycle*)

NARRATOR: Compared with Mrs X, her flocks always came out whiter. Phoebe says:

PHOEBE: This brand always removes marks on my sheep. If I want to do the reverse, I use this brand. (*Mimes seizing red-hot iron*)

CHORUS: (*FX Hiss and shriek as brand is applied to the backside of a sheep*)

NARRATOR: Phoebe knew all her sheep by name.

SHEEP 1: Baaarney.

SHEEP 2: Baaarclay.

SHEEP 3: Baaartholomew.

SHEEP 4: Baaarbara.

SHEEP 5: Laaambert.

SHEEP 6: Eewan.

SHEEP 7: Raaamsay. (*Pause*)

SHEEP 8: (*A more tentative offering*) Shorn?

NARRATOR: And many others. They stayed together and they sang together.

PHOEBE: (*Leading the* CHORUS *in singing the nursery rhyme*)
Baa! Baa! Good sheep will together stay,

CHORUS: Yes, Miss. Yes, Miss, if you say.

PHOEBE: Look for the others,
Never, ever stray,

CHORUS: And don't talk to strangers you meet on the way.

PHOEBE: Now, you can all go off and eat.

NARRATOR: (*Smugly to audience*) But do remember to say *graze*. Sorry. Now, the youngest sheep was extremely enthusiastic. (LAMBERT *comes to the front*) He wanted to be everywhere at once and do everything that the older sheep were doing.

LAMBERT: (*Very quickly*) Hey, can I play? Can I play? Can I play? Can I play?

NARRATOR: He had an irritating way of repeating himself.

LAMBERT: What do you mean? What do you mean?

NARRATOR: Oh, never mind.

LAMBERT: (*Eagerly to the other sheep*) Hey, please can I . . . ?

CHORUS: Shove off! Get knitted!

LAMBERT: But I want . . .

SHEEP 2: Get lost!

LAMBERT: Why?

SHEEP 8: Because we want to finish the sketch.

LAMBERT: (*As actor*) Oh, fine.

NARRATOR: And so, discouraged and dismissed, he strolled off by himself. Far, far away from the protection of the flock. Higher and higher he climbed.

LAMBERT: I don't need the others!

NARRATOR: He cried, slipping on a patch of wet grass.

LAMBERT: I'm quite happy playing by myself!

NARRATOR: He shouted, scrabbling at the rock face.

LAMBERT: I want to be alone!

NARRATOR: He shrieked, stepping on a loose clod of earth.

LAMBERT: I wish I could fly!

NARRATOR: He commented, reaching the bottom of a ravine. That night the shepherdess counted the sheep.

PHOEBE: One, two, three, four, five, six . . . (*She drifts off to sleep*)

NARRATOR: She never found this easy. (*He wakes* PHOEBE *up*) Eventually, she finished.

PHOEBE: All right! Where's Lambert?

CHORUS: (*Variously*) I dunno. He'll turn up sooner or later. Shouldn't bother about him. Yeah, bit of peace and quiet for a change.

PHOEBE: But you're supposed to look after him! He's only little.

SHEEP 1: Little so-and-so.

PHOEBE: Why did he run off?

SHEEP 4: 'Cos Baaarclay told him to get lost.

CHORUS: (*Massive groan*) Oooohhh, Baaarclay!

SHEEP 2: (*Who is often persecuted as the form idiot, defensively*) It was only a figure of speech.

PHOEBE: Don't you realise there are lions out there?

CHORUS: L-L-L-Lions!

PHOEBE: And what do lions eat?

SHEEP 3: Lion bars?

PHOEBE: Lambs! You fools!

CHORUS: L-L-L-Lambs!

NARRATOR: So off she ran, leaving the other sheep safely in the fold. There was no time to lose. (PHOEBE *runs round the audience*) She ran through the valley, calling his name.

PHOEBE: Lambert! Lambert! Lambert! (*Fading into the distance*)

NARRATOR: Meanwhile, in the ravine, Lambert was a sitting duck. (LAMBERT *tries to cover his face with a large, yellow beak*) However, this disguise did not fool the lion.

CHORUS: (*FX Lion roar*)

NARRATOR: (*During this speech, the* CHORUS *create the lion*) He was the meanest, wildest, hungriest lion in the land. He had the longest mane, the biggest eyes and was the fastest jaw in the West.

CHORUS: (*Loud roar*)

NARRATOR: The lion prepared himself for dinner. He covered himself with butter and jumped into the oven. He had a very low IQ. At this moment he saw Lambert and emerged from the oven, roaring ferociously.

CHORUS: Ferociously!

NARRATOR: Lambert shared his deep concern about this situation with the rest of the flock.

LAMBERT: (*Yelling*) Aaaaargghh!

CHORUS: (*Together in a deep voice*) Hello, little lamb.

LAMBERT: Pleased to meet you, Mr Lion.

CHORUS: Meat? Did you say *meat*?

LAMBERT: (*Hastily*) No. I was just thinking what a

lovely day it was for a picnic . . . er, *picture*. Taking *pictures*.

CHORUS: (*Working the jaws*) You mean *snaps*?

LAMBERT: No. No, no. I was talking about the weather. I'm roasting . . . er, *resting*, ha, ha, ha . . . er, for a moment in these lovely greens . . . er, green surroundings.

CHORUS: Oh, dear, little lamb, you're all by yourself. What a shame. No pudding.

NARRATOR: Lambert's last moment had come. The lion licked his lips and prepared to leap on Lambert.

PHOEBE: (*Off*) Lambert! Lambert! Lambert! (*Getting louder*)

CHORUS: Whassat?

PHOEBE: (*Entering, she sees* LAMBERT) Lambert!

CHORUS: Oh, good. Pudding!

PHOEBE: Not so fast, Pusscat! (*She does a lightning change of costume á la Wonder Woman*)

CHORUS: Oh, No! Not Shepherd 'S'!

NARRATOR: She gave him a friendly wave. (PHOEBE *thumps lion between the eyes*)

CHORUS: (*Grunt*)

NARRATOR: Showed him the way out. (PHOEBE *gives the lion a kung fu kick in the jaw*) and finally they parted company. (*The lion falls apart*)

CHORUS: (*Led by* LAMBERT, *FX Cheer!*)

NARRATOR: Lambert and the shepherdess were joyfully reunited. She picked him up, tucked him under her arm and, leaping lightly from crag to crag, she skipped over twenty-five miles back to the fold and was instantly selected for Hull Kingston Rovers.

CHORUS: (*Applause*)

NARRATOR: So there they were, back in the fold, to the great delight of all the other sheep.

CHORUS: (*Feebly*) Hooray.

NARRATOR: Now, come on, I want to hear a proper cheer from everyone.

CHORUS: (*Still without any enthusiasm*) Hooray!

NARRATOR: Unless I hear a proper cheer, this whole sketch is in detention!

CHORUS: (*Wildly*) HOORAAAY!

NARRATOR: All right, settle down. Now, what's the point of the story? Lambert?

LAMBERT: I was lost but now I'm found.

NARRATOR: Good. Phoebe?

PHOEBE: I rejoice more in finding one lost sheep than I do over all the ninety-nine who stayed at home.

NARRATOR: Excellent. Sheep?

CHORUS: Umm . . . errr . . .

NARRATOR: (*Wearily*) Oh, never mind. Just read the words on the card.
(*He holds up placard*)

CHORUS: The Lord is my Shepherd,
He gives me everything I need,
For ever and ever. Baa-aa-men.

GOOD FRIDAY

Good Friday seems more like 'Bad Friday' to many children, listening to the graphic story of the scourging and Crucifixion of Jesus. It was a day when the sky went black, Jesus died a cruel death and his friends deserted him. It seems strange to remember this as a 'good day', but Good Friday has this name in the sense of 'Holy Friday', just as Christmas time used to be known as the 'good tide'. It is a day set apart for a special commemoration of the Passion. Originally the liturgical colour of the day was black, appropriate for a day of mourning; now it is red to signify redemption. It has generally been a day of fasting, penitence and meditation upon the cross. It is the only day in the whole year, apart from Holy Saturday, when the Mass is not celebrated in the Roman Catholic Church; it is also a day when some Protestant churches place particular emphasis on administrating the Lord's Supper. Either way, it has been regarded as having great solemnity and importance throughout Christendom. In the Greek Church, the day is known as the 'Great Friday'. This is, perhaps, the best name of all, because on this day God reversed all expectations and brought the utmost triumph out of the most terrible desolation.

In view of the mood of most services on Good Friday, performing a sketch is a matter for very careful consideration. Some might argue that a mime like 'The Light of the World' (cf. *Time to Act*) is the most appropriate kind of material. We have included a sketch that takes a very unusual look at Good Friday and shows more clearly than most why we should rightly refer to this day as 'Good Friday'. It sees the Crucifixion through the eyes of the thief on the cross, to whom Jesus said, 'This day you shall be with me in Paradise'. Although the sketch is written about Good Friday, it can be performed throughout Holy Week and, indeed, it has been performed on the stage and broadcast on BBC radio at many different times of the year.

The Newcomer

WING COMMANDER LUMINOUS, *an angel*; FLYING OFFICER CUMULUS, *an angel*; THIEF

The two angels stand by the reception desk in Paradise (clearly marked 'Reception'). They are wearing costumes which are a combination of angelic garb and RAF uniform, with the appropriate stripes according to rank. In the original production, LUMINOUS was male and CUMULUS female, and this is preserved in the stage directions here.

LUMINOUS *scans the horizon, off-stage right, through binoculars.*

CUMULUS: Gosh, Commander, who do you think it's going to be? Maybe a Roman emperor or a king or a famous poet!

LUMINOUS: Possibly. It's certainly going to be somebody mighty special.

CUMULUS: Just think – the first person to arrive in Paradise after the gates have been thrown open. What a privilege!

LUMINOUS: Stand to attention, Flying Officer, here he comes!
(*Enter* THIEF, *ragged, unwashed, wiping his nose on his sleeve. He gazes all around, amazed*)

THIEF: 'E weren't jokin' neither!
(*The angels exchange glances*)

LUMINOUS: Sorry, sir?

THIEF: 'E weren't joking' about 'is kingdom an' that!

CUMULUS: I beg your pardon?

THIEF: This is Paradise, in it, Guv?

CUMULUS: Yes.
(*The angels cough nervously*)
THIEF: Terrific, eh?
LUMINOUS: Er . . . We like it, sir.
THIEF: Like it! Do us a favour, this is fantastic!
Look at them trees towerin' like a
thousand feet high, wiv every leaf
shimmerin' like a gold bar an' all that
stuff. (*There is an uneasy pause.*
LUMINOUS *shuffles through his papers,
then looks up*)
LUMINOUS: Do you have any credentials, sir?
THIEF: Wot?
LUMINOUS: Papers? Identification? A certificate of
approval?
THIEF: Gorra copy of me death warrant. Any
good?
LUMINOUS: I – I think there's been some mistake.
CUMULUS: What my colleague means is, er, what
have you *done* in your life that might
give you entrance to . . .
THIEF: Done? You mean done in?
LUMINOUS: I'm sorry?
THIEF: Done *in*. I mean, I've done in a few
people, worked 'em over. Done a bit of
blag, y'know, a few good earners,
robberies wiv violence, GBH. Yeah, I
been around in my time, but never seen
no place like this.
(LUMINOUS *takes* CUMULUS *aside. He
talks urgently*)
LUMINOUS: Who is responsible for checking in the
newcomers at the gate? Aren't you
supposed to be on duty, Flying Officer?
CUMULUS: With respect, Commander, my duty is
next millenium.
LUMINOUS: Well, even though *technically* the doors
are now wide open, there's still got to be

somebody doing a spot of eternal
vigilance. Now we've got a gate-crasher
at the banquet!

THIEF: Look at them flowers like diamonds! I
tell yer, if I'd known about this place
and seen all this gear, I wouldn't 'ave
bothered wiv that job on Pontius
Pilate's country residence. No way, I'd
'ave been up 'ere an' ripped this place
off. And, yet, funny in it – all them
lovely things an' that, an' I 'aven't put
one in me pocket. I ask yer, me! Ron
the Con. It's a laugh, in it?

LUMINOUS: What did you say your name was?

THIEF: Ron the Con. Get it? Y'know. Tony the
Phony. Bill the Kill.

CUMULUS: (*Gulping*) Did you say . . . Bill the Kill?

THIEF: Yeah, told yer, I done me fair share,
then I got pulled in – I got lumbered,
didn't I? Well, I ask yer, I didn't know it
were Pontius' joint, did I? Course, it
were crawlin' wiv Roman filth, weren't
it? The whole flippin' ninth legion, no
less, an' so I got me collar felt.

LUMINOUS: You had what?

THIEF: Are you deaf or summat? I was sussed,
weren't I? Wiv the bung in me hand, the
jewels an' that – wiv me dagger still
fresh from the job, drippin' wiv blood
all over the shop.

CUMULUS: You killed someone with your dagger?

THIEF: Well, I didn't tickle 'im under the chin.
What's up wiv you lot?

LUMINOUS: (*Panicking*) I'm sorry. There's been a
dreadful administrative error.

CUMULUS: But just suppose, Commander –

LUMINOUS: Suppose what!

CUMULUS: That *we* have made a dreadful error.

LUMINOUS: Impossible. Angels do not make errors.

CUMULUS: Lucifer made a pretty big one.

LUMINOUS: Now look here! Are you saying –

CUMULUS: I'm just saying that, well, there are things which even angels do not understand yet – maybe –

LUMINOUS: You're not trying to tell me that all these trumpets and hallelujahs and splendid apparel and gallivanting around rejoicing and banqueting all over the place are for the benefit of a common criminal! It's outrageous! It's back to front! I – I'm sorry, I can't believe this. I shall have to go to the top and get official verification. (*Exit*)

CUMULUS: But, Commander – don't leave me on my own, he might be dangerous! (*Turns round nervously and bumps into* THIEF. *She jumps*) Ah, still here, are you?

THIEF: Yeah, I thought I'd 'ave a look round.

CUMULUS: Oh well, that's nice. Good. Um. May I ask who sent you here?

THIEF: Funny you should ask that. I don't know 'is name, actually. I think it was something beginnin' wiv J. He were on the cross next to me.

CUMULUS: (*Suddenly, she realises. Awed*) You mean – the Lamb of God, the Holy One, the Prince of Peace!

THIEF: No, not any of those, it was – Jesus, that's it. That was the feller's name. (*She bows low in adoration of Christ*) 'Ere, what's up wiv you, got stomach cramp or something?

CUMULUS: O blessed Lord – may glory be given to your name! (*She continues to pray and worship as* THIEF *talks*)

THIEF: Jesus! Yeah, that was his name and –

funny thing – it sounds like music, as I
says it, like a strange song from another
country . . . 'Jesus' . . . There we were
both dyin', only me for me crimes an'
that, caught at it – got me deserts – but
'im, what 'ad 'e done? Nothing. I could
see that, couldn't I? Do us a favour. I
thought, what's a poor Charlie like that
wind up on death row for? Then I knew
– 'e were no ordinary geezer. There was
something about 'im. Fear. I saw it – not
in 'im, no! – in *them*, religious leaders
an' that. They were in a right funk,
weren't they? Knees knockin'! I saw
their game – they were standing around
watchin' to check 'e didn't leap off. I kid
you not! Now who ever leapt off a cross,
eh? Give us a break. Different, 'e were,
talkin' about 'is kingdom! Mumblin',
people weepin', holdin' on to 'is feet an'
'im talkin' about comin' into 'is
kingdom! I said, 'Listen, mate,
remember me when you get into that
kingdom.' Then 'e looked at me, you
never seen nothin' like them eyes –
lookin', searchin', probin' into me soul.
An' then he speaks to me – straight out,
bang to rights – he says, 'This day you
shall be wiv me in Paradise.' (*Pause*)
That were the nicest thing anyone had
said to me all day. 'Paradise? Where's
that?' I says. An' 'e said nothin'. 'E
smiled. In that agony, 'e smiled. I didn't
know where Paradise were an' that, but
if 'e were gonna be there, I wanted to be
in on the act, know what I mean?
(LUMINOUS *rushes back and seizes*
CUMULUS *by the arm*)

LUMINOUS: This is very embarrassing!

CUMULUS: (*Who is still spellbound*) I know.

LUMINOUS: We've committed a terrible faux pas!

CUMULUS: I know, isn't it wonderful?

LUMINOUS: Wonderful! I've just gone and made a fool of myself with the Archangel Gabriel! I said, 'There's been a dreadful mistake, this man's a common criminal, he's nobody special at all!' And Gabriel said, 'Well, he is now.' And I said, 'Whaaat?' Then he said, 'What's your definition of special?' And before I had time to reply, he said he thought 'a personal invitation to Paradise from the Lord of Life made a person quite special enough, thank you very much.' Then all the seraphim laughed their heads off. I tell you, if angels could blush, I would have gone golden. (*Turning to* THIEF) Your Grace, I really do apologise for any inconvenience that my vacillations may have caused.

THIEF: Wot?

LUMINOUS: (*Producing magnificent robes*) Please try these for size.

THIEF: 'Ere, what's all the fab gear for then, eh?

LUMINOUS: (*As both angels dress* THIEF) The banquet. You're the guest of honour.

THIEF: Somebody's birthday, is it?

LUMINOUS: Yes, yours. Incredible, isn't it? The last person shall be first, and the first shall be last!

CUMULUS: Blessed be the lord of Hosts!

LUMINOUS: Amen! His wisdom is infinite!

CUMULUS: There is no limit to his mercy!

LUMINOUS: Hallelujah! His love is everlasting!

CUMULUS: Give thanks to his glorious name!

LUMINOUS: In fact, the more hopeless, the better it is! It's a pretty amazing thing, this 'Gospel'!!

THIEF: Gospel? What's that?

LUMINOUS: Er, well, strictly speaking, it's really justification by faith through –

THIEF: Just if you what?

LUMINOUS: (*Anxiously turning to* CUMULUS) We're going to have to do something about explaining this to people, you know.

CUMULUS: We may well have to rethink our theology.

THIEF: I can't see what zoology's got to do wiv it, mate. I was bein' executed for me crimes an' now I've landed up in Paradise. It's flippin' marvellous!

LUMINOUS: Flippin' marvellous, yes, that's quite a good way of putting it.

CUMULUS: (*Laughing*) Flippin' marvellous! (*They all laugh*)

LUMINOUS: Hallelujah, praise the Lord, it's flippin' marvellous!

EASTER

Easter is the earliest, and the greatest Christian festival. If all other celebrations were forgotten, this one would perfectly express the joy and the hope of the Christian faith. Yet, if Easter were abandoned, all others would lose their significance. The earliest liturgical year was simply a regular celebration of the Easter message, every Sunday, reaching its climax at Eastertide and Pentecost. The early Church was truly a Church of the Resurrection faith: it celebrated Easter, not merely as a commemoration of past events, but as a daily reality and a future hope. It drew deeply from the symbolism of the Jewish Passover – the *pesach* in Hebrew, from which the word 'pasch' and the season of 'paschaltide' come. Anyone who reads Exodus will see that the Passover originated from the Angel of Death, passing over the houses of Israelites whose doorposts had been sprinkled with the blood of a sacrificial lamb. Yet the Jewish feast of Passover was never limited to remembering the past. As well as being a feast of thanksgiving for the deliverance from the plagues of Egypt, it spoke of liberation and the journey into the promised land. Centuries later, the Jews in Babylonian captivity celebrated the Passover with renewed longing for deliverance, and by the time of Christ the Passover festival had taken on an air of fervent expectation: the belief in the promised messiah, who would deliver Israel from bondage and usher in the Kingdom of God.

It was no coincidence that Jesus chose to bridge the gap between the old paschal meal and the coming celebration of Easter with his celebration of the Passover, known to Christians as 'The Last Supper'. This was the beginning of a new age, a new dawn, that would literally begin with the rising of the sun on Easter morning. Easter, today, is a celebration of Christ's resurrection, its meaning for the past, and future of Christendom. The vigil on Easter Eve, always celebrated by the Eastern Church, now recovered by the West, is a waiting for the dawn of Easter Day and, by inference, a waiting for the return of Christ.

The timing of the Easter festival is symbolic of renewal. It falls between March 21st and April 25th, according to the lunar calendar, and coincides with the coming of spring. The evidence seems to indicate that, as with Christmas, the early Christians took over a pagan festival and transformed it into a celebration of the spiritual new life. The derivation of the word 'Easter' has been regarded since the time of the Venerable Bede as belonging to an Anglo-Saxon goddess of spring 'Oestre', although there are some scholars who believe the name may come from a Germanic root, 'Oesteren', meaning 'dawn'. Either way, it seems likely that the Christian Easter not only took upon itself the beginning of the Jewish Passover but also the aspirations of pagan religions expressed in the spring festivals. This can teach us something today about taking the hopes of the world and giving them new life and meaning in the context of resurrection joy.

Easter also had another vital role in the early Church, which was the baptism of new converts. Lent was a preparation for the catechumen of fasting, penitence and prayer, leading to the Easter vigil (all night long) and the awesome moment of baptism at the dawn of the new day. The practice of infant baptism, among other factors, led to the disappearance of this custom, but it is surely a worthwhile association for all Christians. Easter is the birth of the Church; the message of death and resurrection is repeated in every Christian who dies to himself and rises into union with Christ; and even if we do not perform baptism at Easter, it is the time for renewing our baptismal vows.

Finally, as regards some of the more bizarre customs associated with Easter, particularly the giving of Easter eggs (which almost certainly belongs to the pagan festivals), these can be appreciated as a way of making the greatest occasion in the Church's year become special in the minds of children, even though there are some dangers. A nephew (aged 4) of one of the authors had the following comment to make about the festival: 'I love Easter, especially the big ones.' Perhaps, one day, he may transfer his emotions to the realisation that the Resurrection is the biggest event in human history . . . The two sketches that follow, aim to make this clear.

Many Happy Returns

NARRATOR; MARY MAGDALENE; PETER; JOHN; JAMES; THOMAS;
JESUS

The text given here is intended as an outline for a group improvisation around the Resurrection appearances of Jesus as they are described in St John's Gospel. It is offered as a theatrical experiment which your group may like to make. The actors should treat the dialogue as a series of suggestions to help them express their own thoughts and feelings. As with any 'performed' improvisation, its success depends upon the work each actor has done before the scene opens; mentally developing the background to the different characters and imaginatively getting inside the mood of the occasion. The audience should feel that they are watching an extract from a much longer play; the action has already begun. In the sections where the disciples are arguing together, aim for a reality in the dialogue – the edges may be blurred, people talking over each other, not finishing their sentences, etc. Each disciple has a different attitude to the events. They all wear modern working clothes.

We have suggested using a few of the disciples who would have been together on that first Easter morning. You may wish to include some others, depending on the size of your group, though too many will tend to make the improvisation clumsy. PETER *and* JOHN *are sitting together downstage.* MARY MAGDALENE *enters hurriedly as the* NARRATOR *speaks and looks into 'the tomb' upstage.*

> NARRATOR: Early on Sunday morning, while it was
> still dark, Mary Magdalene went to the
> tomb and saw that the stone had been
> taken away from the entrance. She ran
> and told Simon Peter and the other

disciple whom Jesus loved. (MARY *turns and runs downstage towards* PETER *and* JOHN. *She arrives breathless and almost hysterical*)

MARY: They have taken the Lord and we don't know where they have put him!

PETER: That's impossible. It would take eight men to move that stone!

MARY: I'm telling you, he's not there! The stone has been rolled back and the grave is empty!

JOHN: Why should anyone have taken him away? There's no reason to.

PETER: Maybe the priests –

JOHN: But why set a guard over the tomb and watch it for two days?

PETER: Mary, are you dreaming?

MARY: (*Shouting, close to tears*) Go and see for yourself! The tomb is empty!

JOHN: This is crazy – it's not possible!

PETER: (*Getting up*) Come on! (*They run offstage*)
(MARY *is left alone. She turns upstage and sits on a rostrum, weeping.* JESUS *has entered quietly and is sitting behind her and slightly above*)

JESUS: Woman, why are you crying?

MARY: They have taken my Lord away and I don't know where they have put him.

JESUS: (*Speaking softly*) Who is it that you are looking for?

MARY: (*Without looking up*) You must be the gardener, sir. Please help me. If you took him away, tell me where you have put him and I will go and get him. (JESUS *gazes at her with the compassion and humour of a parent whose child weeps over nothing. Almost as a rebuke, he speaks her name*)

JESUS: Mary.
(*Very slowly* MARY *raises her face from her hands. Her lips begin to move, but we hear nothing. Slowly she turns round and looks at* JESUS. *The truth dawns on her. Suddenly, as if waking from a dream, she flings her arms round him*)

MARY: Master!
(JESUS *accepts her embrace and then tenderly lifts her to her feet*)

JESUS: Don't hold on to me now, because I have not yet gone back to the Father. But go to my brothers and tell them, I am going back to him who is my Father and your Father, my God and your God.
(*She looks at him, hardly able to take in the beauty of this promise. She is reluctant to let his physical presence go. Gently, he takes her hands away*)

JESUS: Go now. (*She turns to go, hesitates and then turns back, but* JESUS *has already 'vanished'. Throughout the following scene,* JESUS *remains onstage. The disciples see him appear and disappear though he is always in full view for the audience*)

MARY: (*Softly*) Lord! . . . Lord! (*Suddenly, filled with joy, she begins to run offstage. She shouts*) Jesus!

(*Immediately, we hear the other disciples arguing together. They enter in the middle of a heated discussion, carrying a large fishing net between them. They walk past* JESUS *without seeing him and settle down to mend the net. The first few*

*lines of the improvisation may be heard
offstage*)

PETER: How do we know that Mary isn't
imagining things? She's been very upset
and now she's having comforting
dreams.

JOHN: What comfort is there in a lie?

PETER: Well, if it's real to her!

JAMES: But what good is it to us? We saw him
die like any other person that's ever
died!

JOHN: Then why is the grave empty?

JAMES: I'll tell you why it's empty.

JOHN: Go on, tell me.

JAMES: The Pharisees have taken the body for
safe-keeping.

JOHN: Without the graveclothes? Who could
possibly –

JAMES: That's just another of Mary's
hallucinations –

JOHN: Look, we went there!

PETER: But I don't understand, why would the
Pharisees leave an empty tomb to
spread rumours about the Messiah
rising again?

JOHN: The Pharisees know it's empty and they
still haven't produced the body.

JAMES: So we've all got to start believing Mary,
is that it?

PETER: There must be an explanation! Mend
the net.
(JESUS *walks over to the group*)

JESUS: (*Cheerfully*) Peace be with you.

JAMES: (*Without recognising him*) Oh, peace be
with you, too.
(JESUS *sits down with them and joins in
mending the net. He is in the middle of
explaining to them a good way to patch a*

hole, when they all fall silent and stare at him)

JESUS: No, no, don't be afraid. (*He breaks the silence with a laugh*) Look at my hands and my feet. Here, feel me. A ghost doesn't have flesh and bones. (*He smiles. For a moment no one dares to speak*) Have you anything to eat? (*Now the disciples can relax. They begin to laugh and talk. One of them hands* JESUS *something to eat. Suddenly,* JESUS *'vanishes'. They are stunned for an instant and then begin excitedly to improvise their reactions*)

PETER: He was here. He was sitting down just there!

JOHN: It was him!

JAMES: It was the Lord! He said, 'Give me something to eat'! (*They catch sight of* MARY *who is leading* THOMAS *over to them*) Thomas! Thomas, we have seen the Lord!

PETER: Thomas, we saw him with our own eyes!

JOHN: He was sitting here!

THOMAS: How many more times are we going to hear this, 'We have seen the Lord! We have seen the Lord!'?

JAMES: Are you saying you don't believe us?

THOMAS: (*Sarcastically*) Well, when Mary saw him it wasn't true, but now that James has seen him, of course –

JOHN: Mary saw him in the garden. We saw him here. Others have seen him outside Jerusalem. Why should –

THOMAS: Look, I doubt everything which I don't see for myself.

JOHN: Why should we all lie?

THOMAS: Well, supposing you were? Supposing

everyone was deluded? Does that make
it right for me to believe a lie?

PETER: Why are you so stubborn?

THOMAS: Because I'm not crazy, that's why!
Because I'm not a fool or a madman!

JAMES: Didn't you love him?

THOMAS: (*Vehemently*) Of course I loved him!
We all loved him! But now you're
saying he's walking around and talking
with you. Don't you think *I* want that? I
want that for myself! If I'm going to
believe, I want to be so sure that I will
never doubt again!

JOHN: What's going to convince you, Thomas?

JAMES: What's going to make you so sure?

THOMAS: I'll tell you what's going to make me
sure. Unless I see the scars of the nails
in his hands and put my fingers where
the nails were and my hand in his side,
I will NOT BELIEVE!
(*He leaves them abruptly, walking to the
other side of the stage.* JESUS *gets up and
approaches him*)

JESUS: Peace be with you.
(THOMAS *turns and is utterly astonished.
He trembles*)
Look at my hands. Put your finger here.
(*Lifting his shirt*) Stretch out your hand.
(THOMAS *reaches forward*) Now, stop
your doubting and believe. (THOMAS
collapses onto his knees)

THOMAS: My Lord and my God! (JESUS *hugs him*)

JESUS: Do you say this because you see me?
Happy are those who believe in me
without seeing me!

*The basic text reproduced here is an extract from a full-
length dramatisation of St John's Gospel, first produced at*

the 1984 York Festival by Riding Lights Theatre Company. The production was staged in St Michael-le-Belfrey Church and then toured to major theatres around Britain in the spring and autumn of 1985.

World Exclusive

KOWALSKI, *a newspaper editor*; VINCENT, *a reporter*

It is easy to lose the impact of the gospel in over-familiarity. In a way, this is the dilemma of Western Europe and America: the extravagant claims that a man rose from the dead have been absorbed into our cultural heritage; the shock has been neutralised. Suppose, however, that there were newspapers in Rome when the story first reached the West . . . this sketch follows on from this premise, in a parody of the Hollywood 'front-page' movie. Actors and directors can imaginatively develop the anachronisms of dress, setting and behaviour as much as they wish. The piece covers a number of arguments for the historicity of the Resurrection and can therefore act as a kind of discussion-starter; it can also be cut down, if required, for a particular context.

Editor's office of the Roman Times, AD 100. KOWALSKI *wears a toga, sunshield, and smokes a cigar.* VINCENT *wears a leather tunic, thick black glasses, and carries a selection of feathers in his top pocket.*

	(KOWALSKI *paces round his office*)
KOWALSKI:	(*Shouting off*) Vincent! Vincent!
	(*Enter Vincent*)
VINCENT:	You called, Mr Kowalski?
KOWALSKI:	(*Abruptly charming*) Oh, thank you, Vincent.
VINCENT:	Sir?
KOWALSKI:	For deigning to grace this office with your imposing presence.
VINCENT:	Sir?
KOWALSKI:	Are you sure that the world's greatest

investigative reporter has got five minutes to spare?

VINCENT: Sir?

KOWALSKI: SIR, SIR! – DON'T SIR ME, SHUTUPANDSIDDOWN!
(VINCENT *sits down*)

VINCENT: I don't understand, Mr Kowalski.

KOWALSKI: You don't understand. I don't understand. That's two of us. Let's hope that somebody round here understands, otherwise tonight's city edition of the *Roman Times* is going into the bucket!
(*He hurls a bunch of documents into the bin.* VINCENT *rises*)

VINCENT: I'd stake my life on that story, Mr Kowalski!

KOWALSKI: (*Leaning over his desk and staring* VINCENT *in the eye*) I've a good mind to take you up on that, Vincent. (VINCENT *sits down*) I send my best reporter to the Colosseum. I want a story on the execution of some religious freaks. I want some details of the cult's activities in Rome. Some personal info. Maybe a few last words. What do I get? Some ridiculous cock-and-bull story about the founder rising from the dead!
(*Bearing down on* VINCENT) Do you think our readership has a collective IQ of 12?

VINCENT: No, sir.

KOWALSKI: This is a serious newspaper. It has a reputation throughout the Roman Empire. The merest hint of an exposé in the *Roman Times* and there is a cabinet reshuffle! A world exclusive and rival publications are queuing up in the bankruptcy courts!

VINCENT: Yes, sir.

KOWALSKI: (*Imitating*) Yes, sir; No, sir; DON'T SIR ME!

VINCENT: But Mr Kowalski, I promise you, this *is* a world exclusive.

KOWALSKI: (*Wheedling*) 'Mr Kowalski, I promise you, this is a world exclusive!' Don't make me cry. This is a piece of junk. (*Picking a sheet of paper from the bin and reading*) 'Man Risen From The Dead', 'The Claim That This Leader Is Alive Today Is Well Substantiated'!

VINCENT: The evidence is outstandingly good, Mr Kowalski . . .
(VINCENT *collects the rest of the file from the bin*)
Have you read the documents?

KOWALSKI: Have I read the – ? What do you take me for, a lecturer in comparative religion? Am I a historical researcher or what? Do I go round reading thick wadges of theological mumbo-jumbo when I have an evening edition to get out by five? You've got five minutes to convince me that this is the biggest scoop in the history of the world, otherwise I'll have your ENTRAILS ON TOAST!

VINCENT: Thank you, sir, thank you. I knew you had an open mind!

KOWALSKI: That's four minutes, fifty seconds.
(VINCENT *takes out a sheaf from the file and lays it on the desk*)

VINCENT: Jesus Christ. A prophet. Politically controversial. Okay?

KOWALSKI: So what's new?

VINCENT: He got executed.

KOWALSKI: You don't say.

VINCENT: (*Producing another sheaf*) Crucifixion. There were many witnesses, Jews and Romans. Dead beyond any doubt. That's important.

KOWALSKI: Why?

VINCENT: Because dead men don't reappear.

KOWALSKI: I'm gripped by this story, Vincent. Four minutes.

VINCENT: Three days later, he shows up.

KOWALSKI: Okay, so it's a hallucination.

VINCENT: To five hundred people at once?

KOWALSKI: I grant you, that's unusual.

VINCENT: (*Throwing down a pile of papers*) Eyewitness accounts. (*Sorting out one*) Most of the five hundred people were still alive when this letter was written to Corinth. Some are still alive today.

KOWALSKI: So a group suffers from mass hypnosis.

VINCENT: The evidence suggests that no one was expecting it. Hallucinations usually occur to people in certain emotional states. A mother sees her dead son at the window. A dying man sees a mirage in the desert. People of unstable temperaments, or in certain special conditions, have hallucinations. But this Jesus appeared to fishermen and tax-collectors, individuals, groups, on roads, in houses, beside lakes, at all times of the day and night!

KOWALSKI: So all these religious fruitcakes wanted to see their leader again. They imagined it. It's a touching story. But it won't make the front page.

VINCENT: (*Leaning forward earnestly*) Hear me out.

KOWALSKI: I'm spellbound. You've got three

minutes, twenty seconds.

VINCENT: (*Getting up and wandering round the office*) So what is the possible explanation? The tomb is empty. There is no doubt about that. It was in the interests of the Jewish authorities to produce that body, squash the rumours and quell the riot! Okay. It stands to reason. But no body. Why?

KOWALSKI: (*Shrugging*) Some dickhead went and stole it.

VINCENT: (*Wheeling round*) Who?

KOWALSKI: A disciple, I dunno. I'm asking the questions, jerk!

VINCENT: You think those Christians go to their deaths, proclaiming the resurrection of Christ, when they all know the body of their leader is rotting in a Palestinian grave?

KOWALSKI: So the body disappeared. Hey presto! No body. It's a freak. An omen. A religious curiosity, but it ain't front-page news.

VINCENT: I'm coming to that. The front-page bit is the claim that this guy – Jesus – was God!

(KOWALSKI *jumps up and shuts the door*)

KOWALSKI: (*Turning*) Keep your voice down, Dumbo! The emperor's a bit touchy about his own claims to be God.

VINCENT: Sorry, Mr Kowalski. I realise that this is a political hot potato.

KOWALSKI: Hot potato, my grandmother! Get to the point before the Imperial Guard bust us all for high treason! You've got two minutes, forty seconds.

VINCENT: Hallucination won't explain it. Stealing the body won't explain it. The

KOWALSKI: imagination of his followers won't explain it – the last and most dramatic appearance was to a Jewish Pharisee.

KOWALSKI: What the heck is that?

VINCENT: A fanatical sect, observers of the law down to the last letter. Totally, utterly opposed to the Christ sect.

KOWALSKI: And one of these parsnip guys meets Jesus?

VINCENT: On the road to Damascus, years after his execution.

KOWALSKI: It's creepy.

VINCENT: Guy named Saul of Tarsus, a Roman citizen.

KOWALSKI: A what?

VINCENT: An educated man, an intellectual! Kapow! His whole life is changed. He goes round preaching the Resurrection and, a few years ago, he gets executed, about a mile from here, singing hymns and talking to Jesus.

KOWALSKI: (*Pause*) Are you sure this guy was a Roman citizen?

VINCENT: Here's his file.

KOWALSKI: Letters?

VINCENT: Epistles to churches all over Asia.

KOWALSKI: (*Sifting through*) You've done your homework, Vincent, I'll say that for you.

VINCENT: Four eyewitness accounts of the death and resurrection of Jesus.

KOWALSKI: (*Reading*) Gospels . . . (*Suddenly*) This could be a load of baloney.

VINCENT: The way I figure it, those guys are speaking the truth.

KOWALSKI: (*Pushing the Gospels aside*) I ain't gonna be screwed up with no forgeries, Vincent – remember the Nero Diaries!

VINCENT: That's just the point, sir, the Nero Diaries were copies clean out of a history book. But there are *four* Gospels. And they have crucial differences. Now if witnesses in a court of law all told a story, word for word the same, their testimony would be false. It would be plain as daylight, they were all spinning exactly the same line. These are independent testimonies, seen from different points of view.

KOWALSKI: Hold it, hold it! You mean the evidence is contradictory?

VINCENT: No, sir. It all builds a whole picture. Like Hannibal crossing the Alps. Livy says he took one route and Polybius says he took a completely different route. Two famous historians – but nobody doubts that Hannibal made it to the other side. Beside, all the Gospels clearly agree on the essential facts – this man Jesus died, was buried and rose again, and was seen by hundreds of witnesses.

KOWALSKI: (*Swallowing a mouthful of pills*) Why do you do this to me, Vincent? How do I know that these aren't the cleverest fakes that have ever been made?

VINCENT: One good reason, sir. They're the worst fakes that have ever been made.

KOWALSKI: Vincent. You are crazy as nutbar. One moment you're saying that these are the truth, and the next that they're the worst fakes that have ever been made.

VINCENT: Exactly, Mr Kowalski. No Jew is gonna make the first witness of the Resurrection a woman. Her testimony is invalid in a court of law.

KOWALSKI: That's heavy.

VINCENT: So why do that? Unless it was true?

KOWALSKI: I know you got a master in journalism, Vincent, but why can't you pick some ordinary stories for a change like 'Priest of Dionysius Hacks Vestal Virgin to Pieces'? Something normal.

VINCENT: (*Oblivious*) And there's another thing – any self-respecting forger is going to claim that he saw the event himself, make it sound more authentic. Like signing a fake picture. It stands to reason. But nobody actually claims to have seen the Resurrection itself. And the men saw Christ *after* the women. (*Triumphantly*) It doesn't make sense, unless it makes sense!

KOWALSKI: You've lost me there, Vincent. (VINCENT *tries to explain*) No, don't bother!! Enough of all the legal mishmash, you've gotta admit, this was probably one stupendous hoax.

VINCENT: Stupendous is not the word for it, Mr Kowalski. I'd say it was so incredible, it's absurd. The only valid explanation is that these witnesses are speaking the truth.

KOWALSKI: (*Looking at the Gospels again*) So who are these guys?

VINCENT: Apostles.

KOWALSKI: These guys are letters?

VINCENT: No, Mr Kowalski. Epistles are letters. Apostles are people. First-hand witnesses, chosen by Christ himself.

KOWALSKI: 'Gospels', 'Apostles', 'Epistles' . . . This religion won't get far. It's too confusing.

VINCENT: How much time have I got left?

KOWALSKI: None.

VINCENT: Mr Kowalski, listen to me. Publish this story. If it's true, life will never be the same for anyone.

KOWALSKI: And if it's false, it won't be the same for either of us, because we'll be dead.

VINCENT: Take the risk.

KOWALSKI: (*Putting his arm round him*) Look, son. You've done some good work here. Your brain has been doing overtime on a fascinating story.

VINCENT: Thank you, Mr Kowalski.

KOWALSKI: Now, I don't know how to break this gently to you.

VINCENT: Right.

KOWALSKI: So I won't break it gently to you, I'll just tell you.

VINCENT: Okay.

KOWALSKI: You're fired.

VINCENT: I'm fired? (*Pause*) You mean I can't work here any more?

KOWALSKI: That's the gist.

VINCENT: Why's that, Mr Kowalski?

KOWALSKI: Because you've gone wacky, Vincent.

VINCENT: I have?

KOWALSKI: Yeah. Wacky, loopy, ha! ha! Funny up top! Weird! You're a headcase, Vincent! A moron! Bats! Cuckoo! Deranged! A vegetable! Do I make myself clear?

VINCENT: No, Mr Kowalski.

KOWALSKI: SHUTUP!!

VINCENT: (*Collecting up the documents*) So you think this is all just a . . . legend?

KOWALSKI: Vincent, have you ever heard of Isis and Osiris?

VINCENT: Yeah. It's an Egyptian legend, but –
KOWALSKI: SHUTUP! (*Sweetly*) Now, if I read
           some nice little story about some pretty
           little princess finding all the little bits of
           her husband, sewing them all together
           and raising him to life by magic, I tell it
           to my children at bedtime. I don't print
           it on the GODDAM FRONT PAGE
           OF THE NEWSPAPER!
VINCENT: (*Hugging the file close*) But Christ is not
           the same as any of these gods and
           goddesses of fairy tales . . . This man
           lived in Palestine within living memory.
           Our own historian, Tacitus, the Jewish
           historian, Josephus, the governor of
           Bithynia, Pliny, (*He taps his file*) they all
           agree about that. You can read their
           reports! This man walked and talked
           and breathed and died . . .
KOWALSKI: And rose again?
           (*Silence. Opening the door for* VINCENT)
           Listen, Vincent. I have some bad news
           for you. Human beings do not rise from
           the dead.
VINCENT: Who says?
KOWALSKI: It stands to reason.
VINCENT: Why?
KOWALSKI: It's not scientific, Vincent. It's not
           possible. This is AD 100.
VINCENT: There could be a first time. (*Holding up
           the file*) This could be the precedent
           for a new hypothesis about life and
           death.
KOWALSKI: (*Pushing him out*) Goodbye, Vincent.
VINCENT: I still think you're missing a world
           exclusive.
KOWALSKI: Vincent. A world exclusive will stand
           the test of time. This story won't last

twenty-four hours.
(KOWALSKI *slams the door, leans up against it, shaking his head sadly*)

CHRISTIAN AID WEEK

The first Christian Aid Week was held in 1957 and since then an annual campaign has been organised to raise funds for many different kinds of relief work in the Third World. While it is one of the largest organisations involved in this work, Christian Aid is by no means the only one. We have included it here in our calendar as a representative of similar relief work and also because the Week itself has become a national institution. In early May each year, 3,000 local committees call upon the help of 350,000 volunteers to distribute educational leaflets and gift envelopes to every home in Britain. The importance of giving cannot be stressed too strongly, but the week is also an expression of Christian unity as members of all the different church denominations can be seen working together. Christian Aid has no expatriate staff working abroad, but allows local nationals to define their own priorities and apportion the funds accordingly.

Too often in the past, patronising attitudes in the rich West and plain ignorance of the real needs of the Third World have hindered relief work and stifled the flow of giving. Our first sketch is directed at both of these targets and satirises the old image of the pompous pioneer who idiotically assumes that all the problems in developing countries can be solved by having 'a strong man at the helm', who is definitely white and knows how to throw his weight around. But it is *he* who is uneducated, *he* whose sense of responsibility is backward and barely 'developing'. This is why Christian Aid attaches such importance to education as well as to the raising of money. *We* need to be much better informed, much more intelligent about our giving and more prepared to enter imaginatively into the suffering of others through our prayers. For the Christian, giving is not an optional extra out of our surplus, but a vital expression of love and a means of grace. To give abundantly and sacrificially is to experience the joy of heaven.

The second sketch looks at how our national priorities are frequently selfish. Despite events like the Live Aid concert of 1985, the urgency of famine relief is speedily forgotten in the stream of news and confusing information that pours from our television sets.

Initiative

PIONEER, *traditional pillar of the British Empire*; CHIVERS, *his eager assistant, excited by the prospect of his first trip overseas*

This sketch is a deliberate caricature of boneheaded philanthropy. The PIONEER *is a typical product of the English public school and the local Scout group, full of self-importance and an all-consuming thirst for adventure. He is dressed in khaki jacket, shorts and a topi, mopping his brow regularly with a large, spotted handkerchief. As the scene opens, he crawls on to the stage, bearing a rifle. Cautiously, he gets up, pointing his rifle straight ahead. He sees a ladder and stealthily climbs up it, looking out to the audience through binoculars.*

PIONEER: Aha! We can't be far from the borders now, Chivers. Think of it. Ngongaland waiting all these centuries for you and me to pitch up and put things right. (*Pause. He looks behind him*) I say, Chivers? Where's the poor blighter got to? CHIV – ERS?
(*Enter* CHIVERS, *encumbered by a rucksack with pots and pans attached, and carrying two very heavy suitcases*)
Shake a leg, old chap. And careful of all those beads and trinkets, we're going to need those for the natives.

CHIVERS: Are we there yet, sir?

PIONEER: As good as, Chivers. Think of it, Ngongaland at last! The land of promise.

CHIVERS: (CHIVERS *has a great batch of papers with*

him. Sorting one out:) According to this leaflet, sir, Ngongaland is one of the poorest countries in the world.

PIONEER: Never mind that, Chivers, we'll soon change all that.

CHIVERS: Yes, sir. Of course, sir. (*Pause*) How, sir?

PIONEER: Initiative, Chivers.

CHIVERS: Right, sir.

PIONEER: Is that clear?

CHIVERS: No, sir – I mean, yes, sir.

PIONEER: All we've got to do is find the big chief, give him a jolly good transistor radio or something –

CHIVERS: But there aren't any radio stations in Ngongaland, sir.

PIONEER: Precisely. While he's working out what to do with the radio, we'll take over the country.

CHIVERS: Right, sir. (*Pause*) What do we do then, sir?

PIONEER: We take a great deal of initiative, Chivers.

CHIVERS: And what then, sir?

PIONEER: Then? Then we take a great deal more initiative, Chivers.

CHIVERS: Can I make a suggestion, sir?

PIONEER: Of course. Put it in the suggestion box. (CHIVERS *takes out 'Suggestion Box', writes note, puts it in and hands it to* PIONEER. PIONEER *takes note out of box. Pause*) Can you read it for me, I've got the wrong glasses on?

CHIVERS: (*Reading*) Well, sir, in the developing world 760 million people are illiterate and to provide the necessary primary education 1,000 new classrooms need to be built each day and 330,000 teachers

trained each year by AD 2000. So maybe
we could take the initiative of starting
an education programme, possibly using
short-term personnel from overseas . . .

PIONEER: Chivers?

CHIVERS: Yes, sir?

PIONEER: You've really got no idea, have you?

CHIVERS: No, sir.

PIONEER: How on earth are we going to build a
thousand classrooms each day?

CHIVERS: Well, not us personally, sir . . .

PIONEER: And what's more, you start making
these chappies read books and you'll
make them a great deal more
dissatisfied with their present situation,
and before you know where you are,
Chivers, you've got a revolution on your
hands.

CHIVERS: Well, sir, with all due respect, I really
think a revolution is what's needed:
water, housing, technology, agriculture,
health services, commerce . . .

PIONEER: Chivers?

CHIVERS: Yes, sir?

PIONEER: What school did you go to?

CHIVERS: Dame Nora Perkins Academy for
Young Ladies, sir.

PIONEER: I beg your pardon?

CHIVERS: I was the gardener. But I thought my
experience in agriculture would be
valuable overseas.

PIONEER: That's what you thought, is it, Chivers?

CHIVERS: Well . . . yes, sir.

PIONEER: These chappies don't need gardens,
with enormous great forests all round
them, Chivers.

CHIVERS: Well, I only thought . . .

PIONEER: They need fine examples of British

initiative. What's that you're holding?

CHIVERS: A Third World fact file, sir. It says that skills are required in administration, cottage industry, engineering, health, vocational training and *rural development*. That's me, sir.

PIONEER: What had you in mind?

CHIVERS: Geraniums, sir. I'm very good at them.

PIONEER: You blithering idiot, Chivers. People can't eat geraniums.

CHIVERS: They can when they're starving, sir.

PIONEER: From now on, leave all the initiative to me, Chivers. That's an order.

CHIVERS: Right, sir.

PIONEER: What's that sign over there say?

CHIVERS: Folkestone three miles, sir.

PIONEER: Tally ho, Chivers. (*Exeunt*)

The Weather Forecast

BRIAN CLEGG, *a TV 'weather man'*

This sketch hardly requires an introduction. A glance at any weather forecast will give a clear idea of the setting (large maps with appropriate symbols will add a great deal to the effect) and a study of the speech will show that it requires regular updating in certain places. These are indicated within brackets, although the text can be freely adapted in other places. Whoever is introducing the text can take on the role of the TV continuity man or woman, with 'And now a look at the world weather situation with Brian Clegg.'

BRIAN: Thank you, (name). Well, little change, really. The Sudan will continue to suffer a major famine. This will move in from the South-West and not clear up after lunch. For those of you taking a holiday on the South Coast of Britain, don't worry, it won't affect Bournemouth. Refugees will continue to move steadily from Ethiopia to Sudan, fleeing from one place without food to another. As you can imagine, from the satellite picture taken at midday, this all happens well to the South of the Sussex-Kent border. The longer range forecast, then. There will be scattered intervals of political awareness during much of the decade, but these will die out fairly soon after the 1985 Live Aid concert, giving way to (a period of heated discussion within the BBC about censorship, debates about football

violence and teachers' pay.) These will
encourage a change in the prevailing
wind of public concern, and by the end
of the 'eighties, a large number of social
and political factors will have obscured
the clear issues of massive Western
responsibility for the Third World. The
outlook, then, for (1987.) Around the
end of December, an alcoholic haze will
descend, creating a thick blanket of fog
in most people's minds, and some rather
blotchy faces, but this will give way to
some thundery spells in the lavatory and
it's fair to say that most heads will clear
during the first week of January. Over
this period, a few hundred thousand
children will have died of starvation, but
generally speaking this fact will be kept
well away from our television screens,
and we can look forward to a generally
bright and prosperous (1987.) A summary
of the forecast for next year, then. No
rain over much of Africa, but extremely
heavy showers over Wimbledon, Lords
and Old Trafford – so sporting fans,
take your umbrellas. Otherwise, a
generally smug feeling settling over
most of Britain, a warm sensation (for
those who've bought British Telecom
shares) and a good deal of frost forming
in the hearts of our political leaders.
That's all from me, goodnight.

Note. We are indebted to Roger Williamson for the original
idea of this sketch.

ASCENSION DAY

It would be an understatement to say that the ascension of Jesus into heaven must be one of the most difficult events to dramatise in the entire Bible. Another contender for an impossible subject, the Resurrection, can at least be seen through the reactions of the disciples, the Romans and the Pharisees (see our two sketches for Easter). In the case of the Ascension, we are less concerned with the human drama than the theological significance of the event: the transition of the risen Christ, in glory, from this world to the next.

No wonder the original accounts of what happened strained the powers of description – Jesus was 'caught up into the sky', according to St Mark's Gospel, 'and sat down at the right hand of God'; 'He was lifted up', says the book of Acts, 'and a cloud cut him off from their sight'. Many twentieth-century theologians have made a great deal of the primitive cosmology which this story seems to portray: a heaven 'up in the sky', God sitting on a throne, a vertical ascent like a balloon. C. S. Lewis admits that the Ascension account 'presents greater difficulties to the modern mind than any other part of scripture'. Yet he argues (in *Miracles*) that 'you cannot take away the Ascension without putting something in its place.' It is a fundamental part of the narrative, which makes it quite clear that Jesus was not a vision or a phantom, but an objective being, with a glorified body. Only a leave-taking of this dramatic nature, a real departure which left no doubt in the minds of hundreds of witnesses, could impress upon the disciples the need to live their Christian lives without relying upon the physical presence of Jesus. Instead, they were to prepare themselves for the coming of the Holy Spirit at Pentecost. Ascension cannot be dramatised as an event and the attempts of even the greatest painters to depict the scene are faintly comic; for we know little of that other world, and only have the merest hints about the nature of the risen body. One thing we do understand, quite clearly, is that our lives need to be lived day by day without the benefit of resurrection appearances ('Blessed are those who have not seen and yet have believed') and that our reliance is not to be upon the five senses, but upon the Holy Spirit that testifies to the truth in our hearts. Any supernatural experiences or visions are merely a bonus to this foundation of faith, but they are no substitute for it.

The Feast of the Ascension, not surprisingly, is regarded as one of the principal occasions in the Christian year. It comes forty days after Easter and it speaks of Christ in glory, exercising all power in heaven and on earth; it also speaks of the need to live by faith. This is the theme of our mime, 'Absent Without Leave', which recalls some of the moments when followers of Jesus were most dependent upon his physical presence. They had to learn to live their lives in a different way after the Ascension, and no doubt it was frequently a painful experience to those who had known such intimate fellowship. Yet, the teaching of the Bible is clear: deeper knowledge of Christ, and closer fellowship, were possible after Pentecost.

Absent Without Leave

NARRATOR; PEOPLE *for a group mime. The size of the group can suit your own requirements of space, etc., but the minimum is one woman and one man*; JESUS

This outline for a simple mime to illustrate various passages of scripture is similar in style to the popular sketch 'The Light of the World' which can be found in our first book, Time To Act. *Alongside the narration we have suggested some movements and images for the mime, though your group might well like to develop these. The piece also works very well set to music with a recorded narration mixed into the sound-track. Aim for some strong, unfussy mime, punctuated by moments of stillness and building towards a series of 'stills' in the final section. The action takes place around a central trestle-table, sturdy enough to stand on and draped in a shroud of black or grey material. In front of this, centre and stage left, are two benches, which are both seats and steps up on to the table.*

The opening image is of a funeral pyre. The actor playing JESUS *is laid out as a corpse on the table. The* WOMAN *sits on the central bench facing away from the audience. She is bent over the body in an attitude of both grief and exhaustion. The* MAN *kneels on the other side of the table; he, too, is slumped over the body, resting his head on its ankles.*

> NARRATOR: From the very beginning, man has felt
> alone in the world. He has reached out
> to God through prayer,
> (*The man moves down left and kneels in
> an attitude of supplication*) sacrifice,
> (*The woman turns and moves down
> right, offering her gift to the heavens*)
> and obeying commandments.

(*They both turn, marching towards one
another. They turn sharply towards the
audience and bow low. As the actor
playing* JESUS *gets up, facing away from
the audience*)
But if I go, I will send him to you. Lo,
I am with you always, even to the end
of time.'
(*The* PEOPLE *reach up towards the figure
above them but find the way blocked by
a 'solid' wall. They retreat, crouching at
the front of the stage*)
Only God can come closer to man.
(*The figure on the table turns and steps
down. He approaches the* PEOPLE *and
becomes the figure of* JESUS *teaching his
disciples*)
Jesus came into the world to show us
what God is like. For a few years those
who knew him came to depend on him.
(*The* WOMAN *stands and turns towards*
JESUS *from stage right*) Martha said to
Jesus: 'Lord, if you had been here my
brother would not have died!'
(*She raises her fist in anger then sinks to
the floor in anguish*)
Jesus said to her: 'I am the resurrection
and the life. He who believes in me,
even though he dies, yet shall he live.'
(*Tenderly, he lifts her face. She clings on
to his outstretched hand*)
Peter got out of the boat
(*The* MAN *mimes stepping over a
gunwale, stage left*)
and walked on the water and came to
Jesus. But when he saw the wind and
the waves he was afraid
(*He looks around him wildly. In*

desperation he reaches out to JESUS)
and beginning to sink, he cried out:
'Lord, save me!' Jesus immediately
reached out his hand and caught him,
(JESUS *does so*)
saying to him: 'O man of little faith, why
did you doubt?'(*The* MAN *shakes his
head sorrowfully*)
Mary stood weeping outside the tomb.
(*The* WOMAN *holds her head in her hands
and sinks on to the bench centre stage.*
JESUS *sits on the edge of the table behind
her. She faces the audience*)
Jesus said to her: 'Mary.'
(*Very slowly she turns to look up into his
face*)
She turned and knew that it was the
Lord. He said to her: 'Do not hold on to
me, for I have not yet ascended to my
Father.'
(*He gently removes his hand from her
grasp and touches her face. The man
steps up on to the table behind* JESUS *and
walks along it. He stands at the far end,
his back to* JESUS, *arms folded defiantly*)
Thomas said: 'Unless I see in his hands
the print of the nails and place my finger
in the mark of the nails and place my
hand in his side, I will not believe!'
Jesus said to Thomas: 'Peace be with
you.'
(JESUS *presents his outstretched hand to
the* MAN *who touches it and kneels in
shame and worship*)
Jesus said: 'Thomas, blessed are those
who have not seen and yet believe.'
(*As the* MAN *and* WOMAN *both try to hold
on to* JESUS *for as long as possible, he*

turns away from them and walks down left)

Once men had known the presence of God among them, it was the hardest thing to let him go.

(JESUS *is now beyond their outstretched arms. He turns back to speak to them*)

But Jesus said: 'It is to your advantage that I go away, for if I do not go away, the Holy Spirit will not come to you. But if I go, I will send him to you. Lo, I am with you always, even to the end of time.'

(*They continue to look towards him, the* MAN *kneeling on the table, the* WOMAN *sitting on the central bench.* JESUS *turns upstage*)

God is with us, even though we cannot see him.

(*The* PEOPLE *look out into the audience. They create cameo scenes to illustrate the following sequence*)

In love

(*From their positions they turn and gaze adoringly into each other's eyes.* JESUS *stands behind them*)

and separation.

(*The* WOMAN, *still seated, turns violently away from the* MAN *who hangs his head.* JESUS *places a hand on each of them, reassuring them*)

Work,

(*The table becomes a conveyor belt on a production line. The* MAN *stands behind it, facing the audience, repeating a mechanical action. The* WOMAN, *from the other side of the table, receives the product from the* MAN *and adds the next* stage of the operation. JESUS *watches them both from the stage right end of the table*) unemployment.

(*The production line stops suddenly. The* MAN *and the* WOMAN *look dejected.* JESUS *grasps the table in both hands and bows his head in exasperation*)

Faith,

(*With* JESUS *in the centre, they all line up in front of the table and looking purposefully towards the audience stage right, take two confident paces forward; then freeze*)

doubt.

(*The* MAN *and* WOMAN *suddenly shrink from the prospect of their belief and turn outwards and lurch upstage. Their fall is prevented by* JESUS *who grabs them by the arm, upholding them while he continues to look steadfastly in the original direction of 'faith'*)

Freedom of choice.

(JESUS *moves away upstage, stepping on to the table, leaving the others to mime helping themselves to a variety of foods in a canteen*)

Oppression.

(*The* MAN *and* WOMAN *turn back to back and link their arms, struggling against one another.* JESUS, *above them, facing away from the audience crosses his arms behind his back, as if tied at the wrists, and receives a blow to his back*)

Life,

(JESUS *steps down, upstage of the table. The other two spin outwards in a graceful yet energetic movement, expressing vitality. Before the next word*

is spoken, the MAN *moves on to the table,
taking up the same position as the 'dead
man' in the opening image*)
and death.
(*The* WOMAN *bends in grief at the head of
the body*)
Jesus said: 'I am going to prepare a
place for you.'
(*He watches as the* WOMAN *moves to take
up her original position, seated on the
central bench. Her hunched shoulders
tell us that she is sobbing*)
'I will come again and will take you to
myself,
(JESUS *positions himself close to the
body, bracing himself to lift its weight*)
so that you can be with me for ever.'
(*As the final word is spoken,* JESUS
*freezes at the moment when he would lift
the body up. He gazes intently and
lovingly into the dead man's face as he
gathers the body beneath knees and
shoulders. The final 'frame' should be
an image which is both strong and
tender*)

PENTECOST

The word Pentecost is simply the Greek for 'fiftieth' and it denotes the fiftieth day after the Feast of Passover when the Jews gave thanks to God for the harvest.

In the Old Testament there were three main pilgrimage festivals when the male population had to present themselves before the Lord in Jerusalem. The first was the Passover (or Unleavened Bread), the second the Feast of Weeks and thirdly the Feast of Tabernacles. It is the Feast of Weeks which underlies the Christian Feast of Pentecost. First and foremost, it was an agricultural festival when the people came to offer to God the first fruits of the grain harvest and it was, like all harvest festivals, a time of great rejoicing and merrymaking. It was set seven weeks – or fifty days – after the Passover, which was the length of time set aside for harvesting. Jewish tradition also began to associate the Feast of Weeks with the giving of the Law to Moses on Mount Sinai, sealing the Old Covenant which began with the deliverance of the children of Israel from Egypt, remembered at Passover.

The Christian tradition which has been superimposed on all this has several interesting parallels: Christ's triumphant deliverance of mankind from the slavery of sin and death took place at Passover and this New Covenant was sealed by the giving of the Holy Spirit to the apostles on the day of Pentecost, seven weeks later. The first fruits of this new spiritual harvest were the 3,000 souls who were added to the number of believers on that day (Acts 2:41). Like the many others who would have been drunk in Jerusalem at a harvest festival, the apostles were accused of being 'filled with new wine', if rather early in the morning before all the festivities had really got going. But their uninhibited rejoicing was a result of being filled with the Holy Spirit.

In early Church tradition, Pentecost was a feast on which many new converts were baptised, dressed in white robes, which is why the occasion is also known as Whitsun or White Sunday. In medieval England offerings called 'Pentecostals' were made to the parish priest.

The major theme which survives within the celebrations of the modern Church is this giving of the Holy Spirit to the apostles, accompanied by supernatural manifestations and Pentecostal gifts. As Jesus had promised at his Ascension, they were clothed with power and went out boldly on to the streets to preach the gospel. Pentecost was the day on which the Church went public. The day on which the Spirit of Jesus and the power of Jesus were made available to all, reluctant and fearful as they may have been.

Our two sketches for this occasion are deliberately contrasting. The first gives a picture of a modern church rediscovering the true meaning of Pentecost and the variety of gifts given to them by the Holy Spirit. The second provides a warning to those whose personal spirit of triumph and rejoicing makes them insensitive to the problems and despair which others may be experiencing. Spiritual renewal is not a panacea for all suffering; we must learn to weep with those who weep, while gently lifting their eyes towards the love of God.

The Birthday Party

THE HOLY SPIRIT; MEMBERS OF THE CHURCH: FRANK, *the minister;* PAUL *and* ROSIE, *leaders of the youth group;* GORDON, *chairman of the outreach committee;* IRIS, *in charge of catering;* CHRISTINE, *choir leader;* BOB, *lay preacher and travelling evangelist;* DENNIS, *church treasurer*

Pentecost is often called the birthday of the Church. Before his ascension, Jesus commissioned his disciples to 'go into all the world and preach the gospel' but first they were to wait in Jerusalem until they were clothed with 'power from on high'. The book of Acts tells us that they all devoted themselves to prayer in preparation for the coming of the promised Holy Spirit. When that day came, they surged out into the city, full of a new authority and vitality and the Church of Christ was born in a remarkable way. By contrast, the modern Church often seems dispirited and hesitant, shy of its gifts and content to leave most of the work in the hands of a few over-burdened 'professionals'. There is little sense of the body of Christ and a whole range of activities limp along in their own strength. Pentecost is the day which reminds us that this is not the way the Church is meant to function; God longs to clothe us with power again and lead us out into the world.

In this sketch, members of a local church have come together to celebrate their anniversary. There is a 'bubbly' atmosphere at this happy family occasion with a level of laughter that shows they all get on together extremely well. A person representing the Holy Spirit is a kind of master of ceremonies. He or she is dressed distinctively, possibly in white, but is by no means strange and aloof in relating to the other characters. The gifts which are given by the Holy Spirit are brightly coloured boxes of varying shapes and sizes, each labelled for the audience to read then concealed in a wrap-

ping of festive paper. The church members enter and arrange themselves in little groups on the stage, talking and joking.

VOICE: (*Over*) When the day of Pentecost had come, the Church were gathered together in one place. And suddenly – (*Enter* HOLY SPIRIT, *carrying a large birthday cake with eight candles. Everyone quickly joins in the song*)

HOLY SPIRIT: Happy Birthday to you,
Happy Birthday to you,
Happy Birthday dear Church,
Happy Birthday to you.
(*Applause and laughter.* HOLY SPIRIT *gives a candle to each person. They continue humming the tune*)

VOICE: (*Over*) And there appeared to them tongues as of fire, distributed and resting on each one of them. And they were all filled with –
(*The candles are blown out. More cheering and cries of 'Speech!' 'Come on, everyone make a speech!'*)

PAUL: Come on, Frank!

FRANK: (*Beaming*) Well, if we had something a little stronger than ginger beer, I'd ask you all to raise your glasses to another year! Still, another year it has been. (*Pause*) I'd like to say it's been a very good year. I'd like to say that. (*Laughter*) Ha Ha ha! But as you all know we've had our ups and downs, thinking of Jennifer's long illness. (*Sympathetic murmurs*) However, there *have* been one or two signs of encouragement. We've held our usual services, of course, each week and our usual many, many meetings (*General groans*), but I'm sure I don't need to reiterate them all for you now. Still, as I say, another good year and, well . . . someone else? Paul? Or perhaps it's Rosie? Sorry. Rosie. (*He sits down*)

ROSIE: (*She has pages of notes and starts rather self-consciously*) Apparently –

PAUL: Sock it to 'em, gal!

ROSIE: Apparently, I'm doing this one.

PAUL: She's the boss.

ROSIE: Shut up, you. So, um . . . there's not a lot to tell you all, really. The youth group's been ticking over quite nicely. Attendances have been a little down, but we think that's probably due to a lot of our young folk going away to college and one thing and another. But, um, yes, we're generally pretty pleased. (*She begins to sit*)

PAUL: Barbecue.

ROSIE: Oh, yes. You're all welcome to come along to the barbecue on Saturday.

PAUL: Bring your own sausages.

FRANK: Thank you. Who's next? Outreach. Gordon.

GORDON: (*He doesn't get up*) Outreach, yeah. Well, we decided against doing the outreach again this summer. The weather's not exactly been brilliant. (*General laughter*) We thought it was more within our limits to do this every other year to start with. If anybody's got any bright ideas for Christmas or anything, they can come and tell me afterwards. And I'll tell them what they can do with their bright ideas! (*More laughter*)

FRANK: Iris, anything to report?

IRIS: No, thank you.

FRANK: Do you still need more helpers?

IRIS: We can *always* do with more helpers! And washer-uppers! (*General groans*) So, come on, you men!

FRANK: How's the choir been, Chris?

CHRISTINE: I think I ought to be asking you that, really! But perhaps I'd better not! (*She laughs*) As you know, we've been trying out a number of new songs recently, which haven't always met with complete success, but things might be a bit different if more people actually came to the *practices*! (*There is a short lull*)

FRANK: Bob?

BOB: What can I say? I was counting up the other day, I think I must have preached 106 sermons this year and given about eighty other talks of various kinds on my travels.

PAUL: (*From the back*) Want a lozenge? (*He gets a good response to this crack*)

BOB: (*Slightly embarrassed by this*) No, thank you. (*He continues rather seriously*) I've been very much aware of the spiritual battle this year. Preaching will always be tough going, unless we are prepared to water the soil with our prayers. (*Murmurs of agreement*) Still, we struggle on.

DENNIS: Is it me, now? The dreaded subject, finance. Or the lack of it! Ha ha ha ha! We just about weathered the mid-year crisis over the rising damp in the lower hall and are just beginning to show a

small surplus, mainly due to the Sale of
Work. But you'll be hearing from me
again in due course.

FRANK: I'm sure we will. Well now! (*He
continues to beam at everyone*) I'm sure
that on this special occasion we'd all like
to thank God, as well, for his presence
with us. Where is he? Has he gone?
(HOLY SPIRIT *has left the stage for a
moment*)

HOLY SPIRIT: (*Off*) Just a minute!

FRANK: Ah, yes. I think he's coming back.
(HOLY SPIRIT *returns with a pile of
presents*) To thank him for all the
blessings of the past year. So, thank
you.

HOLY SPIRIT: And now for the presents! Here we are!
That's for you.

FRANK: Presents? Oh, you shouldn't have!

HOLY SPIRIT: Can't have a birthday without birthday
gifts, can we?

FRANK: We really weren't expecting anything,
you know.

HOLY SPIRIT: I know. Now that's for you (*Distributing
the parcels*), here you are. Something
for everyone.

BOB: You needn't have done this. That's a
very kind thought.
(*They are all a little taken aback and sit
around, holding the gifts, wondering
what to do next*)

BOB: Thank you. (*Awkward pause*)

HOLY SPIRIT: Aren't you going to open them, then?

GORDON: (*Suddenly breaking the ice*) Oh, yes.
Now what have we got here? O-ho, look
at that, *Hospitality*. (*Trying to sound
pleased*) That'll certainly come in
handy, one day. Great. What have you

got, Rosie?

ROSIE: (*Glumly*) *Painting Pictures*.

GORDON: Painting pictures? Hmmn. That's a bit odd.

CHRISTINE: No, it's rather exotic.

PAUL: Suits yer, Rose!

ROSIE: But it's not exactly very *useful*, is it? (*The others are busily unwrapping the gifts.* HOLY SPIRIT *watches them*)

PAUL: (*Loudly*) Oh, no! Not *another* one! Look at that, *Organising*. I've got six of these at home already.

GORDON: Perhaps someone's trying to tell you something, Paul! (*General laughter*)

CHRISTINE: (*Looking at* BOB) Oh, now *that's* nice! Have a look at Bob's *Healing*, everybody! Look!

ROSIE: (*Admiringly*) Oh, Bob! Hold it up.

PAUL: Let's see. (*Everyone expresses their approval*)

FRANK: That's interesting, Bob.

BOB: (*Not so sure*) Ye-es, well, I'm not sure it's really *me*, you know.

GORDON: Course it is. Go on, have a go.

BOB: No, I think I'd better stick to my preaching, thanks.

CHRISTINE: You ought to have this, then. (*Handing over her* 'Preaching') It's no use to me.

PAUL: I thought Bob already had that gift, Chris? (*The ensuing laughter embarrasses* BOB)

IRIS: I don't think I shall open mine just yet, it's got such beautiful wrapping-paper.

GORDON: Come on, then, what are you hiding over there, Frank?

FRANK: I don't know, really. I think it must be some kind of ornament. (*Reading the label*) *Prophecy*. Still, I expect I shall find somewhere to put it. Dennis is being rather sly.

CHRISTINE: Own up, Dennis!

PAUL: Perhaps it's rather *personal*!

DENNIS: No, it's just a funny thing for a church accountant, that's all.

ROSIE: (*Studying it*) *Faith?* Not very birthday-ish!

DENNIS: I could do with a big stick to get some money out of you lot.

FRANK: Well, what an odd selection. You don't suppose we could have got the wrong names, do you?

PAUL: Or the wrong church! (*They all laugh and freeze*)

HOLY SPIRIT: (*Coming forward to relight the candles which have been put back on the cake. Speaking to the audience as this is done*) There are varieties of gifts, but the same Spirit. Varieties of service, but the same Lord. Varieties of working, but the same God who inspires them all. To each is given the manifestation of the Spirit for the common good. Do not neglect the gift you have.
(*Singing quietly*)
Happy Birthday to you,
Happy Birthday to you,
Happy Birthday dear Church,
Happy Birthday to you.
(*He blows out the candles*)

The Comforter

MEG; DOREEN

It is easy to offer false comfort with the very best of intentions. Sometimes our eagerness to show our confidence in God, our desire to walk in the Spirit, leads us, unwittingly, to ride rough-shod over the feelings of others. This sketch characterises an unthinking 'triumphalism', which has nothing to do with true spirituality – one that does not break a 'bruised reed' and knows how to 'bind up the broken-hearted'. The Holy Spirit, that came down in power at Pentecost, did not draw the disciples away from the reality of suffering in the world, but prepared them to face it with courage and with true comfort. It is salutary to be reminded of this at a time when Pentecost can be trivialised to mean shallow emotionalism. It is so much more than this; it is power from on high and the transformation of the human heart, enabling the Church to offer healing and comfort to broken humanity.

MEG, *thirties, lies on a couch in deep depression. Next to her is a telephone. Some distance away, indicating another room, is a table with a telephone. Enter* DOREEN, *a vivacious character, singing 'Thine be the glory, risen conquering Son, Endless is the victory thou o' er death hast won.' She picks up the telephone and dials feverishly.*

> DOREEN: Meg? Hi! It's Doreen.
> MEG: (*Picking up the phone lethargically*) Oh . . . Doreen.
> DOREEN: I was just ringing up to see how you were.
> MEG: Actually, I've been quite –
> DOREEN: That's wonderful. Praise the Lord!

MEG: Depressed actually.

DOREEN: (*Speaking over* MEG) Meg, it's marvellous, you'll never guess, that girl, the one who was always criticising me at work, it's incredible. I rang her this morning. I don't know why. I'm sure it was the Spirit leading me. Something just said to me, 'Ring Wilma.' And I said, 'Not Wilma, surely,' but the voice said, 'Yes, Wilma.' So I picked up the phone, and it turned out that she was really in a terrible trouble, and – you won't believe this – praise the Lord! I was really able to help her. I just had the words. I just knew what to say. It was amazing. She went very quiet. She didn't say much, but I knew that God had really spoken to her. Through me! And I really want to encourage you, Meg, because – anything is possible! – and I don't know why I rang you, but I just felt I had to share this with someone, and the Lord said, 'Meg'. And so that's why I'm ringing you, to really say that the Lord loves you, and he's really caring for you, and I just wanted to see how you were, you know, after all . . . after all the problems . . .

MEG: Oh, yes . . . well . . . It's been a difficult time.

DOREEN: I know, I know. I really do feel for you. But it's wonderful, really, isn't it, the way the Lord meets us when we're really down? He just picks us out of the mud and sets us on a rock.

MEG: (*Hardly hearing* DOREEN) I've been quite depressed ever since . . . my baby died . . .

DOREEN: Meg, you know . . . This may be hard for you to understand at the moment, but perhaps the Lord needed that baby more than you, maybe he had a special purpose in your suffering and if only you could understand, you'd really praise and thank him for everything that happens.

MEG: I can't sleep at night, you know, I keep dreaming of that empty cot.

DOREEN: I've had a lot of problems with dreams, you know, but one day I just felt I should hand them over to the Lord, and the bad dreams just stopped. It was incredible. And I really feel I should share this with you, Meg, just trust the Lord over these dreams. Trust him. Thank him for the dreams. Because even the bad things make us need God. I feel the Lord saying to you, 'Thank me for the dreams and I'll release you.' (MEG *is growing desperate. She is fingering a bottle of sleeping pills, which she has taken from her handbag*)

MEG: Sleeping pills . . . the doctor prescribed them . . .

DOREEN: Meg, the doctor once prescribed tranquillisers for me. After two weeks, I praised the Lord and flushed them down the lavatory.

MEG: I feel I can't pray at the moment.

DOREEN: I had that experience once. I just couldn't pray, and I discovered that there was a blockage. It was a small thing. I just hadn't given my peppermints over to God. I know it sounds silly, but I had this thing about Polos, I was always eating them. I used to smoke before I was a Christian. And these sweets were a substitute. And I thought they were harmless. But they weren't. The peppermints were coming between me and God. And I just knew, one day, that the reason I couldn't pray was those packets of mints in my handbag. So I flushed them down the lavatory. Well, they wouldn't go down at first, so I pushed them round the bend with a brush to make sure they were really out of my life. And it was amazing, from that moment on I felt I could really pray.

MEG: I don't even know if there is a God sometimes . . . after the baby died . . . in the cot . . . no warning . . . my husband said he could never believe in a God who did that to babies . . . and he got angry with me for being a Christian . . . then I got the dreams . . . and I can't pray . . . I keep looking at the bottle of sleeping pills . . . counting them out, looking at them . . .
(MEG *has opened the bottle. She tips out the pills*)

DOREEN: Meg, I've got some wonderful tapes which you should listen to. They're by an American preacher called Charlton Swackhammer. He really believes that praising God changes everything for the better . . . Meg?
(MEG *is pouring the pills into a large tumbler of whisky*)

DOREEN: Meg, I know it's hard for you to really let your grief go, but it's possible to hang on to our problems. God wants us to let them go. This is what Charlton

Swackhammer was saying. He says we
have to try and find something to thank
God for, however small, in every
situation.

(MEG *has put the phone down on the
floor. She swallows the deadly potion,
coughing and spluttering*)

(*Continuous*) Now you're saying that
your husband is angry with God. Well, I
think you can thank God even for that.
Yes. (MEG *splutters*) I know it sounds
crazy. But it's not. Really. You can
thank God that your husband feels
something. It would be far worse if he
didn't even talk about God. You can
praise God that he is thinking about
spiritual things. Why don't you do that,
Meg? It's a small beginning, but if you
could only – learn to rejoice in all
things, and at all times, then the
miracles start to happen!

(MEG *has sunk to the floor. She picks up
the phone, as if in a final attempt to shout
for help, but* DOREEN *cuts in*)

Meg, we've got a wonderful God, he's
so much more wonderful and loving and
caring than you and I realise. If only we
could really praise him and sing
hallelujah!

(MEG *collapses, dead, the phone landing
back on the receiver*)

Meg? Meg? The line seems to have
gone dead . . . Oh well, thank you,
Lord, that you cut off the line just at the
right moment, when there was no more
to be said . . . thank you, thank you . . .

(*She starts singing 'Thine be the glory' as
she dials another number*) Hello? Oh,

Debbie . . . I just had to share
something with you. You remember
that girl in the fellowship who hasn't
been coming recently – you know –
Meg? Yes – lost the baby – yes, well, it's
really incredible, I just felt I should ring
her. The Lord said, 'Ring Meg and
encourage her.' And he just gave me
the right words. I knew he was speaking
to her. She didn't say very much. She
went very quiet. But I knew that God
had really spoken to her through me.
Praise the Lord! And I just wanted to
encourage you, Debbie, because
God . . .
(DOREEN *chatters on, but we can no
longer hear her words*)

(*The following quotations from scripture
can be read by one voice, or by several
different voices*)

VOICE 1: There is a time to weep and a time to
laugh.

VOICE 2: Rejoice with those who rejoice and
weep with those who weep.

VOICE 3: When Jesus saw Mary, the sister of
Lazarus, weeping and the Jews who
came with her also weeping, he was
deeply moved and troubled in spirit and
he said, 'Where have you laid him?'
They said to him, 'Lord, come and see.'
Jesus wept.

VOICE 4: Then Job answered, 'Miserable
comforters are you all! Shall windy
words have an end? I also could speak
as you do, if you were in my place.'

VOICE 5: If I speak in the tongues of men and of
angels, but have not love, I am a noisy

gong or a clanging cymbal. And if I have prophetic powers and understand all mysteries and all knowledge, and if I have faith, so as to remove mountains, but have not love, I am nothing.
(DOREEN *freezes, still holding the phone, chattering away*)

TRINITY SUNDAY

As children, the authors were puzzled by the endless Sundays 'after Trinity' in the Christian calendar. What was this extraordinary event that had so many Sundays named after it? After all, no one made much of Trinity Sunday, let alone gave presents or chocolates (a sure way of impressing its importance upon our youthful minds).

In fact, Trinity Sunday has always been something of a poor relation to the other festivals in the liturgical year. It was not until the Middle Ages that it was widely observed as a feast in honour of the Holy Trinity: but it marks the end of the sequence, beginning with Advent, that traces the life of Christ through the passion story and reaches its climax at Pentecost. Trinity Sunday emphasises the divinity of Christ and teaches the unity of Father, Son and Holy Spirit. It centres on the importance of doctrine. We cannot reduce the life of Christ to a magnificent human drama (despite the attempts of film and stage productions); nor can we trifle with the matter of what Christians may or may not believe (despite the attempts of radical theologians).

The doctrine of the Trinity was undoubtedly a battle-ground in the early Christian centuries: over this issue, and many related subjects, acrimonious disputes arose. However, belief in God, as Father, Son and Holy Spirit, came to be a touchstone of orthodoxy and a vital element both in baptismal catechisms and the formulations of belief expressed in the creeds. Doctrine today is no dry, academic matter for Christians: it is as surely the lifeblood of Christian living as are worship and love. Without sound doctrine, securing the essential foundation of Christian belief, Christianity becomes a chameleon religion which changes colour to suit its surroundings. In this way it can be wedded to political ideologies of the right or left, become an empty middle-class moralism, or simply turn into the worst kind of sentimentalism (let's all be nice to each other). Christ, as risen Lord, is all too easily forgotten in our own eagerness to make him 'contemporary'. One thing is certain. Christ is more contemporary than any of us, and most 'modern' theologians are anything but modern.

A cursory glance at the early history of the Church will show how heresies have changed very little over 2,000 years. We have, therefore, chosen a sketch which concentrates on doctrine – in this case, doctrine within the troubled Anglican Church. Not only recent controversies, but the last twenty years or more, have made this particular branch of Christendom a ripe target for a Trinity Sunday sketch. A book like *Christian Believing*, produced by the Doctrine Commission of the Church of England in 1976, has assumptions typical of our times. The questions asked on the jacket cover – 'What is the nature of Christian belief? Is it the acceptance of a truth handed down from the past and enshrined in the Bible and the creeds? Or is it a free and open search for the truth in the present?' – express a subtle form of propaganda. The weasel-words 'acceptance', 'handed down', 'past', 'enshrined' (with its sense of tombs and relics) are associated with the Bible and the creeds; whereas 'free', 'open', 'search' and 'present' are the attractive alternatives of the way of liberalism. The logical consequence of this way of diluting the importance of doctrine might well be the following sketch.

Taking a Stand

Taking a Stand

DIRECTOR OF ST MARCION'S CHURCH ADVICE BUREAU;
ORDINATION CANDIDATE

*See the introduction to 'The God Slot' for the original
context of this sketch.*

The DIRECTOR *should be of the casually dressed 'trendy vicar'
variety, wearing an inconspicuous dog-collar with a colourful shirt, etc. He has an affable, armchair manner interview-
ing the somewhat diffident, prospective* CANDIDATE *for the
Anglican ministry.*

*The setting is a study with two comfortable chairs by the
fireside. The* DIRECTOR *rises to greet his visitor:*

> DIRECTOR: Do come in, er –
> CANDIDATE: Roger.
> DIRECTOR: Roger. (*They shake hands*) Of course.
> (*He sits down and indicates the other
> chair*) Ordination.
> CANDIDATE: (*Sitting down*) Yes.
> DIRECTOR: Have you been to Marcion's Church
> Advice Bureau before?
> CANDIDATE: No . . . No, I haven't.
> DIRECTOR: Right. Well. How can I describe us?
> We're a sort of – theological surgery.
> People come here with various
> complaints or difficulties, personal
> worries and so on, and we try to
> prescribe a remedy if we can.
> CANDIDATE: Great.
> DIRECTOR: So, how do you feel we can help you?
> CANDIDATE: Well, it's about ordination.
> DIRECTOR: Go on.

CANDIDATE: I've always wanted to be a vicar.

DIRECTOR: Mmmm.

CANDIDATE: Ever since I can remember, I've thought, 'That's what I want to be'.

DIRECTOR: So you've wanted to be ordained for many years?

CANDIDATE: Yes.

DIRECTOR: Good. That's a wonderful thing, in many ways.

CANDIDATE: Yes.

DIRECTOR: Not many people today have such a sense of vocation.

CANDIDATE: No . . . No, they don't.

DIRECTOR: So here you are . . . really at a point of decision, er. . . (*Fighting for the name*) Roger.

CANDIDATE: Yes . . . I feel I should go forward, if I can find a way to . . . (*Pause*) There are so many difficulties, this is really the problem.

DIRECTOR: What sort of difficulties, would you say?

CANDIDATE: Mainly with the Bible.

DIRECTOR: (*Nodding*) Uh-huh. I don't think you should let that stand in your way.

CANDIDATE: Really?

DIRECTOR: No . . . Many ordained ministers have similar problems.

CANDIDATE: What about the miracles?

DIRECTOR: The same goes for the miracles. A lot of church leaders have difficulties with them.

CANDIDATE: So I wouldn't be out on a limb, not believing in the miracles?

DIRECTOR: Not at all.

CANDIDATE: Or in . . . the Resurrection?

DIRECTOR: Well, there again—

CANDIDATE: I've always thought that would be a . . . serious blockage.

DIRECTOR: I think the word 'blockage' is very negative. Perhaps 'constructive problem' is the best. Out of your sincere spiritual pilgrimage, your battle with doubts, comes a tougher sort of faith.

CANDIDATE: Faith in what?

DIRECTOR: Well, primarily in God.

CANDIDATE: Actually, I have a difficulty here as well.

DIRECTOR: You're an atheist?

CANDIDATE: Yes.

DIRECTOR: I see . . .

CANDIDATE: Do you think that this is an insuperable obstacle to being ordained?

DIRECTOR: I don't see why it should be. There are quite a number of clergymen who would identify with you, here.

CANDIDATE: I've been afraid that total disbelief in God might ruin my chances.

DIRECTOR: Not at all. Lack of faith is really the basis of all religious experience.

CANDIDATE: I do have some difficulties with the word 'religious'.

DIRECTOR: So do many of us. I think you can safely substitute 'personal' for that . . . 'personal experience' . . .

CANDIDATE: Well, thank you, you've been a great help, I've been so weighed down with problems: The Bible, miracles, the Resurrection, God, being married to a divorcee, and now I feel –

DIRECTOR: Did you say 'divorcee'?

CANDIDATE: Yes. My wife. She's a divorcee. (*Laughing*) But I thought it hardly worth mentioning in the circumstances.

DIRECTOR: Oh dear.

CANDIDATE: Surely, there's no –

DIRECTOR: I'm sorry to disappoint you, Roger, but

it's impossible for you to be accepted for ordination.

(*The* DIRECTOR *stands up*)

CANDIDATE: But my wife's first marriage only lasted two weeks. Her husband ran off with another man.

(*Ushering out the bewildered* CANDIDATE)

DIRECTOR: Situations like this are very painful, but the Church does have to take a stand on *some* issues.

HARVEST THANKSGIVING

Harvest Thanksgiving has been a popular service in churches for over a century. The first fruits of the harvest – corn, fruit, vegetables – are laid around the altar. Special hymns are sung and the food is given away to those in need. The twentieth century has added its own practical touch: tins of beans can be seen stacked up against a sheaf of corn or, failing corn, a packet of corn flakes. No doubt supermarket trolleys, laden with prepacked foods, will make their appearance before long. From the point of view of anyone receiving food from the harvest offering, the latter development is to be welcomed. A prize marrow is an impressive gesture, but not necessarily the most useful gift for a bedridden old-age pensioner.

The origin of the festival may well go back to Anglo-Saxon times when Lammas Day, or the 'Loaf Mass', was celebrated on August 1st. Bread was made from the first ripe corn, blessed and eaten at the eucharist. This custom was revived by an Anglican clergyman called Hawker, in the mid-nineteenth century, when he set aside October 1st for a special Sunday to thank God for the harvest. The Church of England service owes much to his innovation, although Christian celebration of harvest was common on the American continent.

Today, the service has taken on a new meaning: not only do we appreciate the blessing of a good harvest, but we thank God for the privilege of having plenty to eat. The famine in Ethiopia and the Sudan has forcibly reminded people in Western countries of their good fortune and their responsibility to those in need. Harvest time, therefore, is a time of rejoicing but it is also a time when we consider the needs of others. We look at the divine command to love our neighbour. In addition to this, there is a strong association with judgment. The parable of the wheat and the tares is one of several stories that treat this theme. One of the best known harvest hymns makes the connection clear:

> Even so, Lord, quickly come
> To thy final Harvest-home;
> Gather thou thy people in,
> Free from sorrow, free from sin.
> There, for ever, purified,
> In thy presence to abide:
> Come, with all thine Angels come
> Raise the glorious Harvest-home.

There are different messages associated with harvest and we have given a choice of two sketches. The piece for Christian Aid Week (p. 102) could also be used here. 'Cain and Abel' (p. 154) looks at the first harvest offering, and stresses the need for a pure heart in giving to the Lord. 'Noah' (p. 142) dramatises one of the most famous Bible stories about judgment. In this version, the emphasis is on God's goodness and mercy to Noah and his family. The tone is comic (as with the Medieval Mystery Plays on Noah) and the idea is to add some fun to a family service which is held in the spirit of the occasion: namely joyful thanksgiving for the mercies of God.

What to do on a Rainy Day
or
The Story of Noah and World Conservation

NARRATOR ONE; NARRATOR TWO; NOAH'S ELDER BROTHER; NOAH; SHEM, *his eldest son;* HAM, *his dullest son;* JAPHETH, *his youngest son;* DEREK, *a rare species;* OTHER ACTORS IN THE MIME.

The format of two narrators presenting a story illustrated by mime has been tried and tested often enough. Here, the style has been developed to give much more of the dialogue to the characters themselves, but the narrated sequences should still be accompanied by simple and imaginative action. Much of this has been left for you to stage. All props and costumes should emphasise the cartoon element of the presentation.

Admittedly, this is a somewhat 'baroque' treatment of one of the best-loved stories in the Bible and for this reason the director may wish to prune some of the more whimsical scenes for the sake of a more straightforward authenticity. However, if you have the time (and the courage) you will find here an epic to suit an epic.

> ONE: The 'Story of Noah'. (*Ancient actor shakily makes his way on to the stage*)
> TWO: Noah was a remarkable man.
> ONE: He was six hundred and fifty years old. (*Still making his way across the stage, the ancient actor dies suddenly*)
> TWO: Ah. Never mind.
> ONE: He had to go sometime.
> TWO: Thank you very much. (*Actor leaves*)
> ONE: However, Noah had a brother.

TWO: Also called Noah.

ONE: Who was only six hundred years old.

TWO: He was the one mentioned in Genesis, chapter six. (*Enter Noah carrying a placard saying, 'Prepare to meet Thy God'*)

ONE: Noah was a blunt man.

TWO: He was dropped as a baby.

ONE: Noah was the least successful preacher in the history of the world.

TWO: But he was very good with animals.

ONE: As a preacher his message was a failure.

TWO: But his techniques were imaginative.

ONE: He turned up to fancy-dress parties.

TWO: Dressed as a coffin.

TWO: He turned up at beach parties.

ONE: Selling umbrellas.

TWO: The crowds flocked to avoid him speaking.

ONE: Soon, even Noah started avoiding himself.

TWO: He looked the other way in the mirror.

ONE: He rang his own doorbell and refused to answer.

TWO: He helped himself to a cup of tea, and then asked for coffee.

ONE: Finally, he went to see his psychiatrist.

TWO: But was surprised to find that he'd already been.

ONE: Noah had reached the end of himself.

TWO: This was it.

ONE: He had failed.

TWO: Totally.

ONE: Utterly.

TWO: Completely.

ONE: But . . .

TWO: He was still . . .

TOGETHER: Very good with animals!

TWO: And God said:

ONE: 'Noah, I've heard you're good with
       animals.'

TWO: And Noah said:

NOAH: 'Yea, Lord, I am also keen on wild
       flowers, but mine earnest desire is to be
       an preacher of thy righteous word.'

ONE: And God said:

TWO: 'Fair enough, Noah, I have seen your
       righteousness.'

NOAH: 'Yet, O Lord, it troubleth me exceeding
       great that my preaching of thy word
       doth fall on stony ground.'

ONE: 'Let me explain, Noah.'

NOAH: 'Speak, Lord, for thy servant is all ears.'

TWO: 'The first problem is your quirky use of
       the Authorised Version, which is highly
       alienating to the modern culture.'

ONE: And Noah said:

NOAH: 'Fair enough, Lord. I picked it up in
       prayer meetings.'

TWO: But God said:

ONE: 'However, that is nothing compared
       with the violence and corruption that
       have hardened men's hearts.

TWO: 'Now listen carefully.'

NOAH: 'Yea, er, yes, Lord.'

ONE: 'I have lost patience with the
       wickedness of mankind.

TWO: 'I have decided to destroy all the human
       race. (NOAH *looks crestfallen*)

ONE: 'Except . . . you and your family. (NOAH
       cheers up)

TWO: 'For you are the only ones on the earth
       who serve me.'

NOAH: 'Lord, you have really encouraged me
       by saying that.'

ONE: And God said:

TWO: 'To be safe, you'll have to build yourself a boat.'

NOAH: 'Right, Lord, a boat.'

ONE: 'A very large boat.'

NOAH: 'Large boat, yup.' (*Making notes*)

TWO: 'In the middle of the desert.'

NOAH: (*Writing*) 'In the middle of the . . . desert. (*He hesitates*) Um, why would that be, Lord?'

ONE: 'Because that's the only way that you and your family can be saved.'

NOAH: 'Aha. I see! (*He obviously doesn't*) Shall I consult my psychiatrist now, or after I've built the boat in the middle of the desert?'

TWO: 'Noah, I am going to cause a mighty flood to cover the whole earth as judgment for man's wickedness.'

NOAH: 'Ah! Flood, desert, boat, float. Yes, I see it all!'

ONE: 'Well, would you go and do it all.'

NOAH: 'Right, Lord.'

TWO: God told Noah to build himself an ark.

HAM: (*Entering with a small painted rainbow*) 'Hey, I've got an arc!'

ONE: Not that sort of arc.

HAM: 'Oh, sorry. Is this for later on?'

TWO: Yes, that's the wrong prop. That comes at the end.

HAM: 'Fine. (*He turns to leave*) I'll keep it out then, shall I?'

ONE: (*Losing patience*) Yes! (*Recovering*) So God told Noah to build himself an –

HAM: (*Shouting from offstage*) 'I'm putting it on the table.'

ONE: AN ARK!

TWO: So Noah set to work with his three sons,

ONE: Shem, (*Enter* SHEM)

TWO: Ham (*Enter* HAM)

ONE: And Japheth. (*Enter* JAPHETH)

TWO: Who wath the youngetht.

ONE: Thank you.

TWO: Jutht my little joke.

ONE: Shut up!

TWO: Thorry.

ONE: Noah got the plans from God.

TWO: It was to be built of gopher wood.

NOAH: (*Making further notes*) 'Gopher wood.'
(HAM *rushes off stage and returns with a
small piece of wood*)

HAM: 'Here you are.'

NOAH: 'What's this?'

HAM: 'It's pine.'

NOAH: 'I said gopher wood.'

HAM: 'I did.'

NOAH: (*Exasperated*) '*GOPHER! Gopher*
wood! (HAM *still looks confused*) Oh,
never mind. You make the tea.'

ONE: So Ham, Shem and Japheth got on with
the building. (*There is a period of
intense activity. The three lads work with
a will, while* NOAH *peers into his
notebook and orders everyone about*)

TWO: Noah did the calculations,

ONE: Shem planed the planks,

TWO: Japheth jigged the joists

ONE: And Ham hammered the nails. (*They
stand back to survey their work*)

TWO: Together they built themselves a tall,
thin structure, not unlike a telegraph
pole.

ONE: So . . . (*More frantic activity*)

TWO: Shem deplaned the planks,

ONE: Japheth rejigged the joists,

TWO: Ham unhammered the nails,

ONE: And Noah was taken off the

calculations altogether.

TOGETHER: But he was very good with animals!
(SHEM, HAM *and* JAPHETH *continue to build the ark.* NOAH *comes downstage to talk to God*)

TWO: And talking of animals,

ONE: God said to Noah:

TWO: 'Hey, Noah, you're good with animals.

ONE: 'Round up two of every species,

TWO: 'Animals, birds and creeping things,

ONE: 'Clean and unclean,

TWO: 'Every kind of creature

ONE: 'And bring them into the ark.'

TWO: And Noah said:

NOAH: 'Lord, I think you may have forgotten
something. The fish. (*Pause*) But on the
other hand, thinking about it, *I* may
have forgotten something which is the
fact that fish can swim . . . and they may
in fact quite enjoy the whole . . . um
. . . experience. So, fine. Yup. I see it
all.'

ONE: And God said:

TWO: 'Well, would you just go and do it all.'

NOAH: 'Right, Lord. I'll be hurrying along
then.' (*Exit* NOAH, *changing his placard
to 'Prepare to meet thy Dog'*) 'Here,
boy! (*Whistling*) Come to Noah. Come
on.' (*His voice fades out off stage*)

ONE: Meanwhile, back at the ark,

TWO: The building continued.

ONE: The whole ark was waterproofed with
boiling pitch.

TWO: Shem held up the brush,

ONE: Japheth held up the ladder

TWO: And Ham held up the progress.

ONE: But in spite of this,

TWO: The ark was finished

ONE: And Noah returned

TWO: Having completed his mighty work of conservation. (*He enters*)

NOAH: 'Save the tiger!'

SHEM: 'Save the badger!'

JAPHETH: 'Save the whale!'

HAM: 'We'll have it tomorrow with a salad.'

ONE: Look, I'm warning you.

HAM: 'Sorry.'

TWO: Noah had collected all the animals.

ONE: The birds of the air,

TWO: The beasts of the field

ONE: And every creeping thing that creeps upon the earth.

ACTOR: (*Gushing*) 'Oooh, Noah, what a *wonderful* ark! Did you make it all yourself?'

TWO: (*Harshly*) Get in!

ONE: Every creature entered the ark.

TWO: The big ones,

ONE: Two by two by two;

TWO: The little ones,

ONE: Two by two by two;

TWO: The tiny ones,

ONE: Two by two by two;

TWO: The tiny weeny ones (HAM *rushes on, accidentally squashing a small but significant species of beetle*),

ONE: Two by two by – splat!

HAM: 'Whoops. Sorry.'

TWO: Here's the net.

ONE: (*Hands it to* HAM) Off you go.

HAM: (*Singing*) 'The animals went in one by one, one by one . . .'

TWO: Get out.

HAM: 'Sorry.' (*Exit*)

ONE: So, finally,

TWO: When they were all in,

ONE: Checked

TWO: And double-checked,

ONE: Stabled,

TWO: Kennelled

ONE: And perched,

TWO: Noah shut the great gopher-wood door.
(*Enter* DEREK, *out of breath. His costume is a bizarre mixture of horse and drying rack. Various items of clean underwear are attached to his outstretched arms*)

DEREK: 'Hey, wait for me!'

NOAH: (*Wearily*) 'Who are you?'

DEREK: 'I'm a rare species.'

NOAH: (*Consulting his inventory*) 'What are you called?'

DEREK: 'Derek.'

NOAH: 'No, what's the species called?'

DEREK: 'I'm a kind of horse.'

NOAH: 'Sorry. We've got horses.'

DEREK: 'Not a clothes-horse.'

NOAH: 'Look, we've got a full quota of clean and unclean animals. Which are you?'

DEREK: 'Well, most of these are clean, except for the socks.'

NOAH: 'Have you got a mate?'

DEREK: 'Nope.'

NOAH: 'We only have two of everything on here.'

DEREK: 'You could always cross me with something. Cross these with your pandas and you'd get a pair of underpandas.'

NOAH: 'Very funny.'

DEREK: 'Well, I just thought I'd air it with you.'

NOAH: 'Sorry, you can't come in with jokes like that.'

DEREK: 'Oh, go on. I've just tumble-dried all these.'

NOAH: 'Oh, all right.'

ONE: And the door was finally shut.

TWO: Outside, crowds of people in sunglasses,

ONE: Sipping lemonade,

TWO: Mocked and jeered

ONE: Until . . .

TWO: Rumble, rumble.

ONE: Storm clouds approached,

TWO: The sky darkened,

ONE: The horizon vanished,

TWO: Torrential rain lashed the desert.

ONE: Empty riverbeds were engulfed in foaming waters

TWO: And the sale of choc ices fell off.

ONE: Splat!

TWO: Thank you.

ONE: And the people cried out to Noah:

TWO: (*'Burbling' his lips with his hand*) 'Hey! Noah! Any chance of a late booking?'

ONE: (*Also burbling*) 'I believe! I believe . . . I believe that I'm drowning!'

TWO: But the door was shut.

ONE: And the ark rose high above the land.

TWO: For forty days

ONE: And forty nights

TWO: It was carried on the waters of the flood.

ONE: Inside the ark

TWO: It was cosy,

ONE: It was dry,

TWO: It was warm.

ONE: (*Holding nose*) Too warm.

TWO: It was extremely close

ONE: And Noah opened all the portholes

TWO: And noticed that the rain had stopped.

ONE: He let out a great whoop,

TWO: But it couldn't swim,

ONE: So he tried a raven.

TWO: That couldn't swim either,

ONE: But it could fly,

TWO: And it flew back and forth across the water

ONE: Looking for dry land.

TWO: After several more attempts with various birds,

ONE: Noah tried a chicken,

TWO: Which was absolutely delicious.

ONE: His last attempt was a dove,

TWO: Which returned to the ark carrying an olive branch.

ONE: He knew that the waters had abated.

TWO: He called to his family:

NOAH: (*In the immortal style of Long John Silver*) 'HAHAHAHAHAHA! Shem lad! Shiver me timbers, we're home and dry!'

ONE: Noah took a clean pair of animals

TWO: And put them on.

ONE: But they were far too tight.

TWO: They were Noah constrictors.

TOGETHER: Sorry, sorry. We're very sorry.

ONE: (*Crossing to meet* TWO *centrestage*) Look, shouldn't we just get to the message of the sketch?

TWO: You mean there's a message?

ONE: Of course there is. Weren't you listening during all the important bits? Violence and corruption in the world? Repentance, judgment?

TWO: Oh, that.

ONE: Well, an interesting theological point emerges.

TWO: Really?

ONE: Yes. The Hebrew word for the pitch that sealed the ark is *kopher*.

TWO: Ah, yes. And that has exactly the same root as the Hebrew word for atonement, *kaphar*, if I remember rightly.

ONE: You do remember rightly.

TWO: So the ark,

ONE: Which is a type of the Church,

TWO: Is sealed from the flood of God's judgment

ONE: By the atoning work of Christ.

TWO: *Kaphar*,

ONE: *Kopher*.

TWO: This, of course, has nothing to do with *gopher*.

ONE: No.

TWO: Which is merely a kind of wood

ONE: Without any specific, symbolic value.

TWO: Fine.

ONE: And Noah said:

NOAH: 'You what?'

TOGETHER: But he was very good with animals!

TWO: And he let them all out of the ark.

ONE: Then Noah

TWO: And his family

ONE: Knelt down on top of the mountain

TWO: And thanked God for delivering them from judgment.

ONE: And God said:

TWO: Never again will I curse the ground because of men,

ONE: Even though every inclination of his heart is evil from childhood.

TWO: And never again will I destroy all living creatures as I have done.

ONE: As long as the earth endures,

TWO: Seedtime and harvest,

ONE: Cold and heat,

TWO: Summer and winter,

ONE: Day and night

TWO: Will never cease.

ONE: I will set my rainbow in the clouds.

SHEM: 'Hey, where's the rainbow?'

JAPHETH: 'Somebody brought it on earlier.'

NOAH: 'Ham?'

HAM: 'Yeah?'

NOAH: 'The rainbow.'

HAM: 'What, the one on the table?'

NOAH: 'Yes.'

TWO: And whenever the rainbow appears in the clouds . . .

ONE: (*Firmly*) And whenever the RAINBOW appears in the clouds . . . (*Exit* HAM, *sheepishly*)

TWO: I will see it.

ONE: I will *see it*! (*Re-enter* HAM *with rainbow*)

TWO: And remember the everlasting covenant (HAM *holds it up above the group*)

ONE: Between God

TWO: And all living creatures

ONE: Of every kind

TWO: On the earth.

Cain and Abel

NARRATOR ONE; NARRATOR TWO; CAIN; ABEL

*The grim story of Cain and Abel is played out in the context
of the first 'Harvest Festival'. The two brothers come with
their offerings to God in thanks for his help in their daily
work. But the quality of their worship is different. The Bible
doesn't tell us the reason why Cain's offering was rejected,
simply that God had 'no regard' for it. God looks upon the
heart; he is more concerned with our attitudes, with the spirit
in which our worship is offered, than in the mere performance of religious duties. For Cain, the rejection of his harvest
offering added fuel to the fire of jealousy and bitterness
towards his brother which he already had. If our relationships are wrong in the Church our worship will be nothing
more than a nasty stench in the nostrils of God.*

ONE: Adam and Eve,

TWO: Remember them?

ONE: Had two sons.

TWO: Not that overpopulation was a risk at
this stage, but they were being sensible.

ONE: The elder was called Cain. (*Enter* CAIN
in gardening gloves and wellies)

TWO: 'By the Lord's help I have acquired a
son,'

ONE: Said his mother.

TWO: So that's what she called him,
'Acquired'.

ONE: But even in those days this sounded a
little pretentious, so they called him
Cain for short.

TWO: It had a certain kind of ring to it.

ONE: Their younger son was called, 'A bell',

TWO: Which had an even better ring to it.
(*Enter* ABEL, *dressed as a shepherd*)

ONE: Abel grew up to be a shepherd.

TWO: Cain, on the other hand, was a tiller of crops.

ONE: A man of the soil.

TWO: A sifter of clods. (*With simple actions the brothers mime their different occupations*)

ONE: Both of them were God-fearing men,

TWO: So when spring came round,

ONE: It was time to offer sacrifices to God in gratitude for all his provision.

TWO: Abel plodded off into the fields and brought back to the altar the best and plumpest little lamb in his flock. (ABEL *eventually catches an unwilling lamb and carries it to the front of the stage*)

ONE: In a tremendous act of praise and thanks to God,

TWO: Abel slit its throat and set fire to it.

ONE: It smelt beautiful. (CAIN *looks on, disgruntled*)

TWO: Younger brothers can be a bit of a pain at times.

ONE: But not to be outdone, Cain plodded off into *his* fields and sorted out a few things from his harvest.

TWO: A bag of sprouts,

ONE: A bit of barley that he didn't want,

TWO: A cauliflower or two,

ONE: The odd Jerusalem artichoke

TWO: And some really quite nice tomatoes.

ONE: The maggot was only a small one. (CAIN *removes it surreptitiously and dumps the whole lot on his fire*)

TWO: For some reason

ONE: Which mystified Cain,

TWO: This lot didn't seem to burn as well as
Abel's.

ONE: And there was something extremely
irritating about the way Abel was
getting into the worship side of things.
(ABEL, *eyes closed, a blissful smile on his
face, waving his arms like a 'holy roller',
is kneeling beside his sacrifice in silent
ecstasy*)

TWO: And the Lord was pleased with Abel
and his offering.

ONE: Well, anybody could see that!

TWO: Cain's stuff wasn't even disappearing. It
was just giving off nasty, yellow fumes
which made his eyes water.

ONE: And the Lord rejected Cain and his
offering.

TWO: That did it.

ONE: Who did God think he was,
discriminating like that?

TWO: Stupid little squirt of a brother. He
made you really si –

ONE: 'Cain,'

TWO: Said God.

ONE: 'Why are you angry?

TWO: 'Why that scowl on your face?

ONE: 'If you had done the right thing,
wouldn't you have been accepted?'
(CAIN *gets up and paces around*)

TWO: Questions. Questions. It's always the
same.

ONE: Thought Cain. (*He goes into his house,
slamming the door*)

TWO: 'Because you have done wrong, sin is
crouching at your door.' (CAIN
cautiously opens his door a few inches)

ONE: 'It wants to get a foot inside

TWO: 'And rule your house. (CAIN *stands*

behind the door, thinking furiously)

ONE: 'But you can resist it.'

TWO: Cain grit his teeth. (*He steps out and approaches* ABEL, *who has been 'frozen' in an attitude of praise*)

ONE: 'Abel?

TWO: (ABEL *turns.* CAIN *smiles*) 'How about a little stroll, eh?

ONE: 'Stretch the old legs a bit?' (*They turn upstage, walking together*)

TWO: And when they were out in the fields,

ONE: Cain turned on his brother and killed him. (CAIN *trips* ABEL. *As* ABEL *falls*, CAIN *picks up a huge rock and lifts it high over his head. They both freeze*)

TWO: Jesus said,

ONE: 'Whoever is angry with his brother without cause

TWO: 'Shall be in danger of judgment.

ONE: 'First be reconciled to your brother

TWO: 'And then come and offer your gift.'

ALL SAINTS' DAY

November 1st, also known as All Hallows Day (from the Old English word for holy man), is a day to celebrate all Christian saints, both known and unknown.

Ironically, but not altogether surprisingly, most people in Britain seem to attach far more significance to All Hallows Eve, or Hallowe'en, the night before. This is a relic of paganism; a time when the darker supernatural influences are supposed to prevail and when spirits from the visible and invisible world 'walk abroad'. The ancient Hallowe'en customs of nut-cracking, bobbing for apples in buckets of water and discovering one's future lover by eating an apple in front of a mirror are now less fashionable than leaping around at parties, somewhat unthinkingly dressed as witches, or being pestered throughout the evening by groups of children banging on the windows and offering 'a trick or a treat'. It is therefore important for Christians to counter this celebration of occultism, however unintentional, by stressing the importance of All Saints' Day – a great feast of witness to the holy lives and courageous faith of men and women throughout the ages of the Christian Church. We could even start a tradition for All Saints' Day parties and encourage our children to dress up as St George or St Margaret Clitheroe, or even the noble Aloysius Lepp, reputedly the patron saint of hopeless cases.

It is generally agreed that the origin of the feast of All Saints dates from the seventh century, when Boniface IV consecrated the Pantheon in Rome (a temple to all the gods) for Christian worship. From then on there was an annual commemoration of 'all saints' on May 13th, though in the ninth century, this date was moved to November 1st. Many martyrs and non-martyrs had gone unrecorded on earth, while some churches, like those in Rome and Antioch, had more martyrs than there were days in the year! This general feast was therefore a good way of not leaving anyone out. It is also a healthy scriptural attitude to the saints, since the New Testament teaches us that every member of the Church is a 'saint'. Veneration of a few *special* saints can lead to the notion that there are 'A' and 'B' teams within the Christian family, when there are just saints and other saints – all sinners and all struggling to live closer to God. Indeed, no one, apart from God, can be holy, but all those who strive to reflect his nature become increasingly like him.

In the more particular use of the word, 'saints' are people who have a powerful testimony to the overwhelming grace of God in their lives and a humble awareness of his presence with them. They often seem so extraordinarily single-minded about their devotion to God, that to others they can appear to be unbalanced. They are faithful servants with remarkable ministries, sometimes the very conscience of a nation.

For our 'saint', we look at the predicament of one man of whom (almost) no one will have heard and whom some might not even consider particularly saintly. He was a man whose Christian conviction led him into suffering, torn between the claim of God upon his life, as he understood that, and the demands of society. Philip Braden's story is perhaps not very remarkable, but he does show the saintly characteristic of standing out from the crowd and he represents many others whose Christian commitment becomes an issue of dissidence within their society. This sketch may encourage you to research and dramatise similar stories.

As a little footnote to the choice of this particular sketch, it is interesting that the next day in the calendar, November 2nd, is All Souls' Day and apparently this became particularly significant between 1914 and 1918 in view of all the useless slaughter of the war in Europe.

No Peace for the Just

COUNCILLOR ONE, *a senior civic official in charge of a military tribunal;* COUNCILLOR TWO, *ex-military man, now a civilian, pompous, with strongly-held views about national security;* PHILIP BRADEN, *a young conscientious objector;* MEN AND WOMEN IN THE PUBLIC GALLERY

In these times, the terrible truth of Jesus's prophecy about the escalation of violence on earth is constantly before us. Almost daily we 'hear of wars and rumours of war', of terrorism and social violence. There are few areas of the world which are free from armed struggle. The appalling spectre of nuclear holocaust haunts us all. The use of force seems to tarnish so many political and social objectives, both just and unjust, such that many people, including Christians, feel confused and compromised. Sometimes, a look back at the past can help to gain a clearer perspective on the present; hence the reason for this particular sketch, which considers pacifism and conscientious objection during the First World War. On the surface, the sketch is about pacifism, though dramatically it is about one individual standing up for his beliefs in the face of extreme social pressure to deny them. Eric Liddell's principle of conscience at the 1924 Olympic Games has been made famous by the film, 'Chariots of Fire', but here it is the conscience of an unknown man from York which is at stake. Eric Liddell became a national hero; Philip Braden became a national outcast, jeered at in the streets and spat on at work. But like Liddell, he stands for all those who have the courage to match their convictions.

The advent of mass conscription during the First World War prompted widespread dissent among conscientious objectors. 'COs' or 'Conchies' all faced military tribunals which might result in prison sentences or being sent to the Front

with the medical or catering corps. They were ostracised by society and dubbed as cowards. *This sketch is closely based on a transcript of one such tribunal in York, which, of course, has a strong tradition of Quakerism and at the time had six Quaker MPs, including Arnold Rowntree of chocolate factory fame. Little of this dialogue is fictitious, which may come as a surprise, but it shows how farcical some of these discussions actually became. We are indebted to a historian friend, Alistair Mack, for the historical research and for introducing us to the subject in his M. Phil. thesis, 'Conscription and Conscientious Objection in Leeds and York during the First World War'.*

COUNCILLORS ONE *and* TWO *are seated behind an imposing table.* PHILIP BRADEN *stands in the dock downstage. As the scene opens, there is the sound of angry conversation from the public gallery, created by the 'extras' dispersed among the audience. Over this hubbub we hear an announcement:*

VOICE OVER:	Nineteen-sixteen. A military tribunal somewhere in the North of England. (*Noisy disturbance continues as the public express their feelings as to what they think should be done to the accused*)
COUNCILLOR ONE:	Order! Order! (*Hammering on bench with gavel*) I refuse to allow . . . ORDER! . . . I refuse to allow the proceedings of this military tribunal to be interrupted by further outbursts.
MAN'S VOICE:	Shoot the scoundrels!
COUNCILLOR ONE:	I have already warned the gallery. Twice.
ANOTHER VOICE:	(*From the back of the hall*) Speak up! (*General laughter*)
COUNCILLOR ONE:	If there's any more of this nonsense, I shall ask the people in the gallery to retire. (*Murmuring subsides*) Philip Braden, you will repeat what you have

just said for the benefit of the tribunal.
You are not in a music hall now, you
know.

BRADEN: (*Clearly and calmly*) I have always been
opposed to war and have held pacifist
views for several years, as my friends
would tell you.

COUNCILLOR
ONE: Can you produce evidence of this?

BRADEN: No, unfortunately. My friends are now
in prison for their conscientious views.

COUNCILLOR
TWO: (*An audible aside to gallery*) Pity they're
not in the trenches then we'd all be rid
of them. (*Cries of 'Hear, hear!' etc.*)

WOMAN'S VOICE: Keep the flag flying!

COUNCILLOR
ONE: (*To* TWO) Please don't encourage them.
Philip Braden, you are applying for
exemption from military service on
conscientious grounds?

BRADEN: I am.

COUNCILLOR
ONE: And what are the grounds of your
conscientious objection?

BRADEN: I am of the Christian faith and believe in
the sixth commandment, 'Thou shalt
not kill.' If I took another man's life, I
should regard myself as a murderer.

COUNCILLOR
TWO: Do you not think that the military are
taking steps to *save* life by destroying
our enemies and thus preventing further
bloodshed?

BRADEN: I don't believe that two blacks will ever
make a white.

COUNCILLOR
TWO: (*Muttering to himself*) I thought this was
about war, not cups of coffee. (*More
general laughter*)

BRADEN: I demand to be taken seriously. My
faith requires me to turn the other
cheek and to love, not hate, my

enemies. I am a follower of Jesus
Christ.

COUNCILLOR ONE: Aren't we all?

BRADEN: (*Trying to remain calm*) Can you
imagine Jesus Christ dressed in khaki,
out in France, thrusting a bayonet into
the body of a German workman? He
forbade violence even at the time of his
own capture and subsequent death!

COUNCILLOR ONE: Never mind about Jesus Christ, we are
talking about you.

BRADEN: Those who live by the sword will die by
the sword. War is futile. It achieves
nothing.

COUNCILLOR TWO: (*Taking a new tack to avoid stalemates*)
Tell me, Mr Braden, do you think it is
right to defend women and children and
old people . . . like the chairman of this
tribunal? (*Laughter from the back*)
Please don't misunderstand me.

BRADEN: I should do all I could to defend him to
the extent of not taking life.

COUNCILLOR TWO: You are not being asked to *take life*.
You are being asked to stand with your
country in upholding international law
. . . policing the world to prevent other
nations running amok and destroying
national freedom.

BRADEN: But police are not a military force. They
do not take life. I would not take life.

COUNCILLOR ONE: Do you not think this country is worth
fighting for?

BRADEN: My conscience would not allow me to
do that. (*Cries of 'Coward!' etc.*)

COUNCILLOR ONE: (*Attempting to be very reasonable*)
Supposing the Germans were about to
rape your mother and sister and you had

a loaded pistol in your hand. What
would you do?

BRADEN: In the first place, I would not have a
loaded pistol in my hand.

COUNCILLOR But supposing you had?
ONE:

BRADEN: It would be quite impossible to suppose
this in view of my beliefs.

COUNCILLOR (*Ploughing on*) Suppose I threw it at
ONE: you just before the Germans entered
your house?

BRADEN: I wouldn't catch it.

COUNCILLOR (*Getting worked up*) What if I threw it at
ONE: your face?

BRADEN: If I saw it coming, I would duck.

COUNCILLOR Not if I threw it quick enough!
ONE:

BRADEN: (*Aware of the farcical nature of this line
of enquiry*) In that case, I would be
knocked unconscious and be in no
position to use it, anyway.

COUNCILLOR That's absurd.
TWO:

BRADEN: So is the question. It's like supposing I
had thirteen legs, would I go on walking
holidays? I would not have thirteen
legs.

COUNCILLOR Stick to the facts.
TWO:

BRADEN: (*Firmly*) Then the fact is, I would not
have such a weapon to hand. I could
only protect my mother and sister by
putting myself in front of them.

COUNCILLOR At the risk of your own life?
ONE:

BRADEN: At the risk of my own life.

COUNCILLOR I thought you said that you were
TWO: opposed to taking life?

BRADEN: I am.

COUNCILLOR TWO: But it's all right to commit suicide, then?

BRADEN: Attempting to protect my mother and sister is not committing suicide.

COUNCILLOR ONE: Without a pistol in front of a pack of bloodthirsty Huns, it is. (*Pause*) Are you in favour of Huns, Ruskies, Gippos, Wops and Argies, Mr Braden?

BRADEN: I am in favour of all human beings.

COUNCILLOR ONE: Dangerous man to have on our side in a crisis, aren't you? Next case.

GUY FAWKES NIGHT

Guy Fawkes Night, or 'Bonfire Night', with its ritual burn-
ings, explosions, Roman candles and Catherine wheels, is
one of the more curious British traditions to survive from
the past. The reasons for all this have been largely forgotten
and we now indulge in a jamboree which is little more than
an excuse to let off vast quantities of fireworks in a few
hours, to light fires in the garden, burn effigies of men
stuffed with combustibles, eat toffee-apples and provoke
small boys to cause all kinds of mayhem with 'bangers'. Few
of us know why we do these things and, if we did, would
probably be less keen to continue them. At most, we know
it has something to do with parliament *not* being blown up
by a man called Guy Fawkes in 1605, and that fireworks
have a vague relationship to barrels of gunpowder in the
vaults of Westminster. We keep 'November 5th' religious-
ly, although its religious significance is completely lost on
us. Here and there, in towns like Lewes in Sussex, the
religious background is preserved and 'bonfire societies'
make a big deal out of organising colourful processions and
ceremonially burning effigies of the Pope as well as of Guy
Fawkes. But the majority, out of ignorance, approach the
occasion more broadmindedly.

Still, in a country which outlaws sectarian violence,
discourages all demonstrations likely to incite social hatred
and that promotes freedom of religious expression, Guy
Fawkes Night should have been suppressed long ago.
Certainly we should not tolerate the lighting of bonfires to
commemorate the persecution of any racial minority. His-
torically, of course, the last-minute discovery of the Gunpowder Plot was an occasion of supreme deliverance. The
King was not assassinated, the government was not des-
troyed and the country was not immediately plunged into

civil war (this happened a few years later). But the country *was* plunged into further years of violent religious persecution. Guy Fawkes, by no means the most important figure in the plot, became a scapegoat for all Protestant hatred against Roman Catholics and the annual celebrations on November 5th therefore became a focus not so much of gratitude for deliverance but of a gleeful ritualising of this hatred.

> Remember, remember the fifth of November.
> The Gunpowder Treason and Plot.
> I see no reason why Gunpowder Treason
> Should ever be forgot.

The old popular song ensured that the tradition was maintained.

This is not the place for a detailed discussion of the complex and rather murky circumstances surrounding the Gunpowder Plot. We must simply remind ourselves that it took place at a time when religion was inseparable from politics and that the man who has entered the English folk memory as the villain with the 'dark lantern and burning match' was one of many dedicated Catholics who despaired of freedom for their faith in a strongly Protestant England. Guy Fawkes came from a respectable family in York and became a Catholic in his early twenties. He had a reputation for piety and bravery and his decision was obviously a courageous one, since to become a Catholic in those days was similar to declaring a Christian faith in a Communist country today. It meant immediate loss of privileges, fines and persecution.

The English Reformation of the sixteenth century is littered with the bodies of both Protestant and Catholic martyrs, as the two sides fought each other for control of the country. By 1581, it was an act of high treason to convert anyone to the Catholic faith. So, the Gunpowder Plot of 1605 was a bold plan by a group of thirteen conspirators to re-establish Catholic control at a stroke. It was to be the catalyst for a national uprising in support of a Catholic claimant to the throne. It was also a plan for an act of outrageous political terrorism on religious grounds. The continuing violence and devastation in Northern Ireland is the modern expression of exactly the same thing, and alone it provides a good reason for not having very much to do with Guy Fawkes Night. If this annual event has anything to teach us at all, it is to remind us that love is the only way to unite people, that oppression causes violence and that persection never solves anything. Our sketch has, therefore, a tenuous connection with Guy Fawkes Night, as such, but points towards the even greater terrors of violence that now threaten our world, unless human beings are prepared to live together in peace.

Every year, public safety films warn us of the dangers of playing around with fireworks. It's a short step to imagine people playing around with other kinds of explosive . . . but you'll have to read the sketch to see what we mean.

Gunpowder Treason

BELCHER, *a teenage devil;* SPITE, *his best friend*

This sketch obviously trades upon the atmosphere of Bonfire Night and it gives a sombre satirical twist to the concept of 'fireworks', but its usefulness need not be limited to November 5th. Its subject lurks at the back of our minds most of the year.

This is a sketch for the production team to go to town on; it requires a whole range of large and brightly-coloured fireworks. Each devil has his own box of them. Only one of these should look like a nuclear weapon: SPITE's *Ultimate Deterrent Banger should resemble a Cruise missile, with fins and some blue touch-paper sticking out of one end. It is his prize possession.* SPITE *and* BELCHER *are both dressed in school uniform – long, dark trousers, blazers, ties, white shirts. They are two typical 14-year-olds and we should think them unremarkable but for the fact that they both sport a pair of stubby red horns.*

As the scene opens, we hear the sounds of fireworks going off, accompanied by the usual gasps, cheers, 'oohs' and 'aahs' of appreciation and disappointment. The sound-track has some specific cues near the beginning which need careful timing. Both devils crouch by their boxes of fireworks. Firelight flickers on their faces. Overhead a rocket whooshes into the sky.

SPITE: Wor! See that one go, Belcher!
BELCHER: Really high. (*There is a loud bang*) Flippin' 'eck! What was that?
SPITE: SS20, must be. Or a Trident. (*A rocket bursts in the sky*) Wheyhey! Meltdown!

(*He watches eagerly*) Red . . . green . . . (*The rocket fizzles out unexpectedly*) Aaaaahhhh.

BELCHER: Still, not bad (*Another rocket goes up*)

SPITE: (*Casually*) 'Nother SS20. Bloke I knew once was muckin' about with a Polaris in his kitchen. Tried to light the wrong end.

BELCHER: Blew his hand off?

SPITE: (*Dismally*) Yeah. And most of South America.

BELCHER: Well, you're not supposed to hold them, are yer? It's got it on it, '*Do not hold in the hand.*'

SPITE: What you got left? Let's have a look.

BELCHER: (*Producing them like items of shopping*) Er, three 'Holocausts', a 'Berlin Candle' and a 'Megaton Whizzofrazzler'. What you got?

SPITE: Two 'Twinkling Cities', a bag of 'Final Flings' . . . and . . . (*Whipping it out*) a 'Moscow Surprise'! And this one. (*He carefully produces his pièce de résistance*) But I'm saving it 'til last.

BELCHER: (*Awestruck*) What's that one?

SPITE: 'Ultimate Deterrent Banger'. It's my last one.

BELCHER: (*Who would obviously like to hold it*) They're great, those!

SPITE: (*Holding it away protectively*) Yeah.

BELCHER: (*After a pause*) Here, why don't we put them all together and bung a match in?

SPITE: What, send the whole lot up?

BELCHER: Yeah, why not?

SPITE: Might be dangerous.

BELCHER: (*With enthusiasm*) Yeah. What's that banger say on it?

SPITE: (*Reading*) 'Light blue touch-paper and
             leave planet.'

BELCHER: Should be okay. Go on then, see what
             happens.

SPITE: We'll get into trouble.

BELCHER: I know. Go on! (*They both chuckle
             nervously.* BELCHER *playfully jogs* SPITE's
             elbow as he tries to pull out a match)

SPITE: (*Chuckling*) Shuttup! Me hands are
             shaking!

BELCHER: Anyway, it's *dark* blue.

SPITE: (*Still trying to light a match*) What is?

BELCHER: The touch-paper. It's *dark* blue, not
             light blue touch-paper. D'you get it? I
             say it's *dark* –

SPITE: Don't.

BELCHER: Some idiots make these things, don't
             they?

SPITE: (*A match flares*) Here it goes, then.
             Watch it!

BELCHER: I will. (SPITE *applies the match to the pile
             of fireworks. There is the sound of an
             enormous nuclear explosion. Over the
             ensuing rumble we hear his voice,
             amazed and fearful*)

SPITE: What are we gonna do next year?

BELCHER: We'll have to find somewhere else (*He
             chuckles*) We could try Mars.

SPITE: No, I fancy a holiday in
             the sun.
             (*They fall about laughing. The lights
             fade*)

REMEMBRANCE DAY

At eleven o'clock on November 11th, 1918, the armistice was signed which brought the First World War to an end. Armistice Day was kept to commemorate all those who gave their lives between 1914 and 1918 and a two-minute silence observed each year at 11 a.m. on November 11th. Traffic came to a standstill in the streets and the whole nation paused to honour the dead. Poppies, sold by the British Legion in aid of ex-servicemen, were worn to recall the poppies surrounding the trenches in the battlefields of Flanders, and wreaths were laid at war memorials all over the country. For the British, the most famous of these is the Cenotaph (literally an 'empty tomb' for those buried elsewhere) in Whitehall, which was dedicated in 1920 to the First World War dead. In 1946 the name was changed to Remembrance Day to include those killed in the Second World War and in 1956 this was fixed as the second Sunday in November.

As our world draws steadily away from these terrible conflicts, this day of remembrance has permanent significance, particularly among younger generations, as a day of prayer for peace. Our choice of 'The Litany of War' for this occasion reflects this. We remember with gratitude the sacrifices of the past and also those whose daily work puts their lives at risk in the present, but, above all, we set our faces towards the future, praying urgently for the peace of the world.

The Litany of War

This piece is an exception within the book. It is not a sketch but a dramatic prayer which may be found to be more appropriate to the mood of a Remembrance Day service. Originally, it was set to music and was the climax to a musical play about the story of Guy Fawkes, first performed in St Michael-le-Belfrey Church, York, in 1980. The play not only told the story of the Gunpowder Plot but exposed the violence and hatred between different groups of Christians at that time. Whatever the issue, whatever the cause, our world continues to cry out for deliverance from the curse of war. As well as praying for peace, we must be prepared to confront the seeds of all violence, whether verbal or physical, in our own hearts and lives.

The litany can be said responsively with a congregation once they have been invited to reply with the prayer, 'Good Lord, deliver us' after each section. It can be led by a single voice, but preferably by a group who may like to experiment with choral speaking, using different voices in various combinations. If the piece is orchestrated in this way, it can become a moving and enriching experience of prayer for the whole congregation. But this needs as careful rehearsing as any sketch. You have it here in its simplest form. The responses are given in italics:

History is never a thing of the past. It is not looking back but looking forward. It is creating good or evil for the future. And now the future of our world hangs over the abyss, suspended like an acrobat gripping on to a rope with his teeth. While philosophers refuse to comment, while politicians qualify every sentence, while preachers hum! and ha! and remind us of three possible ways of seeing everything, from this absurdity

Good Lord, deliver us

For claiming the authority of God for destroying man, made in his image

Good Lord, deliver us

From dividing the body of Christ and from slaying our brothers in the name of Jesus, who gave his life that all men should be as one

Good Lord, deliver us

From the impatience that snatches in the Kingdom of God by force and destroys its virtue

Good Lord, deliver us

From the self-righteousness of governments that proclaim freedom of conscience and persecute those who act differently

Good Lord, deliver us

From the exploitation of human tensions for political gain

Good Lord, deliver us

From the hypocrisy of judges who uphold Christian morality and deny the mercy of Christ

Good Lord, deliver us

From the seeds of dissension in the Church, spreading to the world, giving birth to wars of religion

Good Lord, deliver us

From all religious men that drive nails of oppression into the hands of Christ

Good Lord, deliver us

From all false prophets, from all deceitful orators, from all persuasive tyrants, from all devils masquerading as angels of light

Good Lord, deliver us

From the creeds of war, the injuries of party spirit, the divorce between nations

Good Lord, deliver us

From the stockpiles of resentment

Good Lord, deliver us

From the armaments of pride

Good Lord, deliver us

From the missiles of angry words

Good Lord, deliver us

By the deterrent of love

Good Lord, deliver us

By the revolution of the human heart

Good Lord, deliver us

By the triumph of Christ on the cross

Good Lord, deliver us

From the folly of our own opinions, from the threat of our own desires, from the lusts of our hearts, from the blame that cannot be placed upon anyone but ourselves

Good Lord, deliver us

From the loneliness of sin, from the separation of man from woman, from the disputes between father and son, from the bitterness of politician against politician, from the hatred of people for people, from the madness of mankind and the suicide of the world

Good Lord, deliver us

By the blood of Christ, dropping on the ground during the agony

Good Lord, deliver us

By the blood of Christ, flowing at the scourging

Good Lord, deliver us

By the blood of Christ, gushing forth at the crowning with thorns

Good Lord, deliver us

By the blood of Christ, shed upon the cross

Good Lord, deliver us

By the blood of Christ, the price of our salvation

Good Lord, deliver us

By the blood of Christ, without which there is no pardon

Good Lord, deliver us

By the blood of Christ, river of mercy

Good Lord, deliver us

O Lamb of God, you who take away the sins of the world, spare us, O Lord.
O Lamb of God, you who take away the sins of the world, have mercy upon us.

O Christ hear us
O Christ hear us
O Christ hear us
O Christ hear us
Lord have mercy upon us
Lord have mercy upon us
Christ have mercy upon us
Christ have mercy upon us

From the evil of our times, defend us, O Christ.
Graciously look upon our afflictions
Pitifully behold the sorrow of our hearts
Mercifully forgive the sin of your people

Mercifully lay your hand upon the womb of our century and heal the future. Bring forth children of light
Bring forth ambassadors of peace
Bring forth rulers of humility.

(*Together*) The grace of our Lord Jesus Christ, and the love of God, and the fellowship of the Holy Spirit, be with us all for evermore. Amen.

Note. There is a musical setting for 'The Litany of War', composed by Christopher Norton and available from *Ears and Eyes Music, PO Box TR3, Leeds LS12 2PN*.

The sequence of seven lines beginning 'By the Blood of Christ' is an extract from 'The Litany of the Precious Blood'.

MISSIONARY SUNDAY

Although this is not an official occasion within the Christian year, it has become a firmly established tradition in many local churches from all denominations to set aside a particular Sunday to draw attention to missionary work. The emphasis might be a straightforward call to its own members for increased evangelism in the local community, or a focus upon the work being carried on by missionaries sent out from the congregation. Sometimes one of the many missionary societies might send a speaker to promote its work and inform about the up-to-date needs of various individuals and projects.

The underlying theme of the occasion is much broader than the more traditional idea of Christian work in other countries. Perhaps the very title 'missionary' creates an outmoded image and is a barrier to all members of the church feeling involved in the urgent task of witness? There is a dangerous complacency that lulls us into thinking that Britain cannot be as pagan as anywhere else in the world ('we started this whole missionary business, didn't we?') – hence the need for sketches such as the second one here. But even deeper than this, Missionary Sunday challenges the attitudes of our hearts. Giving money and attending prayer meetings can *sometimes* be a way of keeping Jesus's command to 'preach the gospel' at arm's length. We are not all called to be evangelists, but we are all called to be witnesses and that means being prepared to be public about our faith where we live and where we work, with our friends and our neighbours. The church must never become a ghetto for believers. Paradoxically Missionary Sunday reminds us that every Sunday is a missionary Sunday and every day an opportunity for mission.

The Good Old Ways

TWO MUSIC HALL COMEDIANS; LADY

*A large proportion of this sketch is a song-and-dance routine
which will need careful choreography to ensure that the
words are clearly heard by the audience. The TWO COME-
DIANS should be colourfully dressed in loud jackets, bow ties
and bowler hats or boaters. They should exude energy and
warmth. It is worth mentioning that the final section about
the 'Evangelical Mission to the Poor and Needy' could be
performed without the preceding song-and-dance.*

<blockquote>

(*Enter* TWO MUSIC HALL COMEDIANS)

ONE: I say, I say, I say, do you know what the two things are that I can't stand?

TWO: No, what are the two things that you can't stand?

ONE: The first is prejudice in the Christian Church and the second is yobbos on motor-cycles.
(*'Boom Boom' on percussion*)

TWO: I say, I say, I say, what is the most ridiculous thing I've ever heard?

ONE: I don't know, what is the most ridiculous thing you've ever heard?

TWO: A Christian who hides his light under a bucket.
(*'Boom Boom' on percussion*)
Imagine going to the house of a Christian friend and finding the whole place plunged in darkness.
(*Enter Christian* LADY. *He approaches her*)
Excuse me, dear lady, but where are the

</blockquote>

LADY: lights in your house?

LADY: They're all in the cellar.

TWO: The cellar! Whatever for?

LADY: Well, you see, we're rather embarrassed about them.

TWO: Why's that?

LADY: Ah . . . er . . . when you switch them on, the neighbours can see where we are.

TWO: So don't you ever switch them on?

LADY: Oh yes. We unscrew the bulbs every Sunday and then take them along to a meeting with other people who are embarrassed about their lights, and then we plug them all in and switch them on for an hour.

(*'Boom Boom' on percussion*)

ONE: You're right, that's the most ridiculous thing I've ever heard.

TWO: Not only that, but for some Christians it's a way of life. Maestro, if you please. (*He waves to the pianist. The* LADY *and he now begin their music hall number*)

Oh we don't go in for parties
We don't go into pubs
We don't go in for anything
Like social do's or clubs.

We like to stick together
To shelter from the weather
Of the wicked, wicked world in which
 we live
We like to follow laws
And stay behind our doors
And *talk* about the love that we should
 give.

ONE: Do you know, there are over fifty-three places for social entertainment and

recreation in your town and you don't
go to any of them. So where do you go?

TOGETHER: To Christian meetings of course!

ONE: Meetings! But what do you do for all the
people in the town?

TOGETHER: Do? We pray for them!

We like to stick together
To shelter from the weather
Of the wicked, wicked world in which
    we live
Fighting holy wars
Behind our bolted doors
We *talk* about the love that we should
    give.

TWO: In my street, there are forty-two houses
where they drink beer, smoke
cigarettes, can't control their children
and I'm proud to say, I've never been
invited to any of them.

LADY: In my street, there are twenty-four
houses where people watch violence on
television, wash their cars on Sundays,
read appalling magazines and have
teenage daughters who wear make-up
and I'm more than relieved to say, I've
never been invited to any of them.

Oh we don't go in for gossip
We don't go in for chat
We don't go in for *worldly* friends
Or anyone like that.

ONE: You mean to say, you don't know any of
your neighbours?

TWO: We wave to them in the street.

LADY: And we wish them good morning.

ONE: But what do you *do* for them?

TOGETHER: Do? We pray for them!

We like to stick together
To shelter from the weather
Of the wicked, wicked world in which
   we live
Fighting holy wars
Behind our bolted doors
We *talk* about the love that we should
   give.

TWO: In our home we never play sport on
Sunday, never buy Sunday papers,
never let our children have ice creams
on a Sunday and, I'm proud to say,
never watch television either.

LADY: In our home, it's like Sunday every day
of the week. We don't even have a
television, we never read secular books,
we never gossip with the neighbours,
never have parties and I'm puzzled that
none of our neighbours ever wants to
come to one of our Bible studies.

Oh we don't go in for reaching out
We'd rather drag them in
We don't go in for very much
Except avoiding sin.

We like to stick together
To shelter from the weather
Of the wicked, wicked world in which
   we live
Fighting holy wars
Behind our bolted doors
We *talk* about the love that we should
   give.

ONE: I say, I say, I say, did you hear about the
man who was weeping on the doorstep
of a Christian home because they had
no time for him?

TWO: No, what about the man who was
weeping on the doorstep of a Christian
home because they had no time for
him?

ONE: Jesus came up to him and said, 'I know
exactly how you feel. They haven't had
any time for me for years!'
(*'Boom Boom' on percussion*)
(*A phone rings on a desk to one side of the
stage. The* LADY *answers it*)

LADY: Ah, good morning. This is the
Evangelical Mission to the Poor and
Needy, what can I do for you? . . .
Right, we'll do everything we can to
help you . . . pray for you, send you
money, organise a campaign for you
. . . speak at your meeting, certainly.
Goodbye and God bless you.

ONE: Excuse me, Mrs Fervent, your
daughter's on the other line. She needs
to speak to you urgently.

LADY: Can you tell her to call me back? I can't
speak to her just now.

ONE: She says she's very depressed and needs
to spend some time with you.

LADY: Tell her I'll . . . I'll speak to her this
evening. (*The phone rings*) Hello,
Evangelical Mission to the Poor and
Needy . . . Ah, Mr Zealous, good
morning . . . I'll certainly organise that
rally for you . . . we'd like to give you
every support.

TWO: Excuse me, Mrs Fervent, it's your
next-door neighbour, she's popped in to
ask whether you'd like to come round
for a sherry.

LADY: That's rather awkward. I don't drink
and – oh, my goodness, I'm supposed to

be at the Missionary Prayer Fellowship
– can you put her off?

TWO: She looks a little down . . . spoke of her
husband.

LADY: Oh yes, he left her apparently. Tell her
I'd love to come over sometime in the
near future. (*Back to the phone*) So
sorry about that interruption, Mr
Zealous . . . could you put me on to
Mrs Enthusiasm, I'd be so grateful,
bless you. Hello, Mrs Enthusiasm, this
is the Evangelical Mission to the Poor
and Needy . . . yes, yes . . . bless you
. . . well, I really have appreciated all
your support over the years, and I must
thank you for your generous gifts . . .
Certainly, I'd be more than happy to
speak at the women's group . . . diary's
a bit full . . . what about the fifteenth of
August? Super, bless you, goodbye.

ONE: There's a man at the door who smells of
drink . . . says he lives in the basement
flat over the road . . .

LADY: Just a minute. (*Writing in her diary*)
Fifteenth of August, Women's Group,
3.30 . . . hymns and readings to be
chosen by the seventh of August. Now
look, can you give this man some money
and tell him it's difficult to find any jobs
for him at the moment. (*Phone rings*)
Hello, Evangelical Mission to the
Poor and Needy . . . yes . . . yes . . .
BBC Radio 4! Thought for the Day?
How soon? Fine, I'd love to . . . bless
you, I'll be in touch.

TWO: Another visitor has just called, Mrs
Fervent, but he went away.

LADY: Thank goodness for that. This is getting

ridiculous!

TWO: He left this card. (*Hands it to her*)

LADY: (*Reading*) Jesus called but found you unavailable. (*She is horror-stricken. There is a short silence. The* TWO COMEDIANS *echo the line as the lights fade*)

TWO: Unavailable . . .

ONE: Jesus called . . .

TWO: But found you unavailable . . .

ONE: Unavailable . . .

Note. Music for the 'Good Old Ways' song, composed by Christopher Norton is available on request from *Ears and Eyes Music, PO Box TR3, Leeds LS12 2PN.*

The United African Mission to Britain

INTERVIEWER; REVEREND SAMUEL MZIMBA

This sketch is the final, brief extract from the comedy film WARP, *performed by Riding Lights Theatre Company for Central TV (see also 'The God Slot' and 'Taking a Stand'). It requires one British actor, of any colour, male or female, as the interviewer, but the missionary must not be white. He or she must convincingly represent another nationality for the purposes of the sketch. Depending upon the personnel available, it could equally well be about 'The United Indonesian Mission to Britain', 'The Maori Mission to Britain', or 'The British Inland Mission', founded by the Chinese. It can be freely adapted for the context of a missionary service, above all to stress that missionary work is not something to do with 'overseas' necessarily, but starts at home.*

The format is the typical TV studio interview, with two chairs, a low table with a glass of water and a plant, and perhaps an appropriate backdrop of a map or logo for the programme with the title, 'Focus on Britain'.

INTERVIEWER: Good evening, and welcome to 'Focus on Britain'. My guest today is the Reverend Samuel Mzimba, General Secretary of The United African Mission to Britain.

MZIMBA: Hello.

INTERVIEWER: Dr Mzimba, tell us about your experience as a missionary in Britain.

MZIMBA: It's very hard doing missionary work in a primitive country like Britain.

INTERVIEWER: Why is this?

MZIMBA: Well, famous witch-doctors, like Russell Grant, hold powerful sway over the simple minds of the natives. Many of them are led to believe that they will become bingo millionaires. Others believe that eating natural yoghurt and reading the *Guardian* will lead them to spiritual enlightenment. It is extremely hard for an African to understand these irrational beliefs.

INTERVIEWER: Have you experienced persecution in your mission to Britain?

MZIMBA: Oh yes, it is so easy to offend the gods. For instance, by failing to wear a blue and white scarf in Everton on a Saturday afternoon, or by speaking irreverently of *Coronation Street*. Several of my co-workers have been lost in this way.

INTERVIEWER: Is conversion a possibility in Britain?

MZIMBA: Conversion to a rational faith in God, such as we have known in Africa for many years. It is not easy in a country where people believe that stars millions of light years away will bring them good luck on Tuesday. However, there have been some cases.

INTERVIEWER: Are such people persecuted?

MZIMBA: It depends on the tribal context. In some more powerful tribes, ancestor worship is still common. They believe that because some of their ancestors may have been Christians, they have inherited Christianity and conversion is really a very insulting idea.

INTERVIEWER: Finally, do you have any thoughts about the current doctrinal squabbles in the Church of England?

MZIMBA: In my home country of Tanzania, we have a saying: 'It's a load of –'

INTERVIEWER: (*Interrupting hastily*) Well, that's all we have time for unfortunately, so from myself and the Reverend Mzimba, goodbye.

ADVENT

The Second Coming

The first Sunday in Advent is the beginning of the Christian year, and sets the tone for the whole liturgical calendar. It marks a period of preparation for the coming (Latin, *adventus*) of Christ. Whether or not a particular church uses the liturgy, or places great store by dates and events, it is true to say that all Christians are concerned with the coming of Christ every day of their lives. The fact that Christ has come is the meaning of the Christmas festival; the knowledge that he rose from the dead and comes today through his Holy Spirit to dwell within human hearts, is the meaning of Easter and Pentecost. The certainty that he will return is the belief expressed in all festivals, above all in Advent itself.

So the Christian year, has a remarkable unity, as should the theology and beliefs of Christian people. Yet this is not always so. Some groups of Christians emphasise the second coming in such a way that they fail to live in the present world; some may even be drawn into various 'adventist' movements that frequently have little to do with orthodox Christianity. Even more dangerous, perhaps, are those within the Church who virtually ignore the teaching that Christ will come again as judge at the last day. His advent in glory and majesty can easily be forgotten in the preparation for celebrating his first coming (see sketch 'Getting Ready', at the beginning of the book, p. 35). This is why we have placed the season at the end as well as at the beginning of *Red Letter Days* – for this date, unknown to us, is already marked in the calendar of God.

There are many sketches that could be written to provoke discussion about the second coming of Christ; here is one, based upon a curious true story that set the authors thinking . . .

The Claims of Christ

HENRY, *a partner in a firm of solicitors;* CAROLINE, *another partner in the same firm;* RON, *a bricklayer from London*

On December 18th, 1981, the Daily Mail *carried a bizarre item under the headline, 'Twenty "Christs" claim £30,000'. It read as follows:*

> Twenty people are claiming to be Jesus and the rightful heir to £30,000 left in the will of religious recluse, Ernest Digweed. Mr Digweed was found dead four days ago in the tent in the living-room of his house in Portsmouth. The walls were covered in crosses. He also lived sometimes under piles of deckchairs. He left his entire estate to Jesus so that he would have some money if the second coming should actually occur. But until then Mr Digweed named the Public Trustees as executors and it is they who must decide whether any of the claimants is Jesus. They refuse to reveal the identities of the hopefuls though one is rumoured to be a steel worker from Sheffield. They will not say what the criteria are for checking each claim. An official said, 'We have politely acknowledged all claims. Usually people go away after a while or admit they cannot support the claim. If, however, there was a claim which appeared to be theologically sound, then it would have to be considered very carefully.'

The mind boggles at the idea of a waiting-room full of people posing as the Son of God. What clothes did they choose that morning? Did they come on the Underground? Swap parables while they were waiting? The whole thing is, of course, absurd, not to say mentally deranged – a black pantomime in contrast with the awesome glory of the return of Christ as prophesied by Jesus himself. This sketch takes this newspaper article as a starting-point, but what interested us particularly was the sentence, 'They will not say what the criteria are for checking each claim.' How will we recognise Jesus when he comes? What will happen on that momentous occasion? As it develops, the sketch moves from farce into urgent discussion between two agnostics. They suddenly find themselves facing an issue which is of the utmost consequence to us all.

In order to prepare your audience for the shocking nature of the beginning of the sketch, you may want to refer to the article in the Daily Mail. *To avoid upstaging some of the comedy, we suggest that the introduction should go something like this:*

> 'Twenty "Christs" claim £30,000.' Twenty people are claiming to be Jesus and the rightful heir to £30,000 left in the will of Mr Ernest Digweed, who was found dead four days ago in Portsmouth. He left his entire estate to Jesus so that he should have some money if the second coming should actually occur. Until then, Mr Digweed has named the Public Trustees as executors and it is they who must decide whether any of the claimants is Jesus.

A solicitor's office. CAROLINE *is seated behind a desk, upstage left and* HENRY *is wandering around the room. Various papers and books, including a Bible, are on the desk. There is a second chair stage right.* HENRY *is in mid conversation as the scene opens.*

HENRY: I think we'll just have to wait on that one and see how things go in the courts. (*There is a knock at the door*) Come. (RON *enters in working overalls, eating chips from a newspaper. They both ignore him*) Mind you, with Harrison representing the other party, I doubt if we'll have what you might call *a smooth ride*. (*He sniffs the air*) Is there something cooking in here? Funny smell all of a sudden.

CAROLINE: Hmmn. A distinct whiff of fried potatoes.

HENRY: Horrible. (*Turning to* RON) Sorry about the smell. Yes?

RON: I've come about the money.

HENRY: (*To* CAROLINE) Have we just had the windows cleaned?

RON: Thirty grand.

HENRY: Thirty what?

RON: Thousand nicker.

HENRY: I don't quite follow.

RON: Sorry?

CAROLINE: (*Pleasantly assuming control*) Shall we start again? You seem to be interested in some kind of remuneration.

RON: No, it's about the money.

HENRY: Whose money?

RON: Well, you've got it at the moment, but it's mine. You owe me thirty thousand quid. (*He parks himself in the empty chair*)

HENRY: (*With heavy sarcasm*) American Express all right?

CAROLINE: Is this anything to do with the Ernest Digweed bequest by any chance?

RON: Yeah, that's it, Digweed. That's the feller, yeah.

HENRY: (*Rather pointedly turning his back on* RON *again, he leans on the desk to talk to* CAROLINE) The Ernest Digweed bequest?

CAROLINE: Yes, this has become something of a problem recently, Henry. The late Ernest Digweed left a certain amount of money in his will –

RON: Thirty thousand pounds.

CAROLINE: (*Ignoring this*) And claimants have been flooding into the office ever since. This is number forty-eight.

HENRY: And who was this Mr Digweed?

CAROLINE: I don't know, really. He was found dead in a tent in the living-room of his home in Portsmouth.

HENRY: I see.

CAROLINE: He also made our company executors of his estate and occasionally lived under piles of deckchairs.

RON: Great man. Ahead of his time, you know, Digweed.

HENRY: (*Turning to him*) No doubt. So you are a relative of this Digweed, are you? (*His tone suggests that he hasn't yet forgiven him for the smell of chips*)

RON: Er, no.

CAROLINE: Digweed didn't leave the money to his family.

HENRY: Oh, I see. So he left it to . . . ?

CAROLINE: Jesus Christ.

RON: That's me, yeah.

HENRY: (*After a brief silence*) Sorry, I'll ask that again. He left it to . . . ?

CAROLINE: Jesus Christ, in case he should need ready cash on his return to this earth.

HENRY: A-ha. But if my facts are correct, Jesus Christ hasn't been around for a while, has he?

RON: Not until now, no.

CAROLINE: Though believers do expect him to return.

HENRY: And is that 'in clouds descending' or 'eating a bag of chips'? Sorry, I forget the exact wording.

RON: Well, it's figurative, isn't it?

HENRY: Yes, the main figure being thirty thousand pounds. I see. So, Mr . . . ?

RON: Er, Christ.

HENRY: And your first name?

RON: Ron . . . er, Jesus, yeah. Ron's my second name.

HENRY: Your current address?

RON: Nineteen, Acacia Grove, Wapping.

HENRY: (*To himself*) A divine little suburb.

CAROLINE: Do you have any identification, Mr Christ? Passport? Driving licence?

RON: Not on me, no.

CAROLINE: Can you then perhaps in some other way substantiate your claim to be the king of all creation?

RON: Well, it depends what you mean.

HENRY: (*Struggling to keep his patience*) All this red tape must seem rather strange and unnecessary to you, but you must understand that down here on earth there are certain formalities which we terrestrial beings must negotiate on our weary way.

CAROLINE: Can we get this straight? You have come along here this afternoon expecting to leave with a cheque to the tune of thirty thousand pounds because you claim to be the Son of God. Is that correct?

RON: I'd prefer cash. Fives and tens. Tax problems, you see?

HENRY: I would have thought heaven was the ideal environment for tax exiles. Now look, this little question of identity *is* rather crucial to any settlement.

CAROLINE: Tradition has it, I believe, that your return was to be announced by the

Archangel's Call and the sound of the
Trumpet of God?

RON: (*Momentarily stumped*) Well, you
wouldn't hear it from here. That was
done over the Specific Ocean.

CAROLINE: (*Sharing a look with* HENRY) Also
accompanied by the heavens passing
away, the elements being dissolved with
fire and the earth and the works upon it
being burnt up. But I imagine all this
takes time.

RON: Once I've got the money I could arrange
it, yeah.

CAROLINE: (*Humouring him*) It does sound rather
expensive, yes, but these are the sort of
things we would be looking for, you
see? So, I think at the moment we shall
have to file your claim under 'Pending' –
pending the cataclysm. Good-day, Mr
Messiah. (HENRY *shows him the door.*
CAROLINE *smiles*)

RON: (*Clutching at any straw*) I've done a few
miracles.

CAROLINE: The feeding of the five traffic wardens?

HENRY: (*Escorting* RON *firmly by the elbow*) Yes,
I expect you've got the Sermon on the
Mount off by now, jolly good.

RON: (*Resisting*) Yeah, I could do you a
speech. A bit of moral teaching . . .
'Love thine anemones!'

HENRY: Not just at the moment, thank you.
We're rather busy. (*Pushing him out*)

CAROLINE: Give our regards to Mr Digweed when
you see him.

RON: He's dead!

HENRY: Exactly. I should think you and he get
on rather well. (*Gives* RON *a final shove
off*) My goodness me! I don't *believe* it!

(*Rearranging his tie and generally recomposing himself*) I suppose we keep the money in an apocalyptic shelter while we work out the criteria for checking any claims.

CAROLINE: Very little legal precedent to help us, I'm afraid.

HENRY: (*Staring out of the window*) What would happen if the genuine article did walk through that door?

CAROLINE: It's hypothetical, of course.

HENRY: Of course.

CAROLINE: I didn't mean that. I meant that presumably there wouldn't be any door left to walk through.

HENRY: You're quite up on all this fire and brimstone stuff, aren't you?

CAROLINE: It's not the first time that the Bible's come to the aid of the legal profession. This case has prompted a little research, one way and another.

HENRY: (*Relaxing into the chair. He continues expansively, enjoying this theological whimsy for a moment*) So, what do you make of all this second coming bit, then?

CAROLINE: Seems to depend on what one makes of the first coming, really.

HENRY: (*Wagging his finger gnomically*) He's no easy man to impersonate!

CAROLINE: (*Seriously*) But would we know him well enough to recognise him if he did show up?

HENRY: Aha, yes. (*Suddenly perturbed by this idea*) That's a good point.

CAROLINE: And is he listening to us now discussing it?

HENRY: What? Oh, this is ludicrous! We can't

seriously be discussing the return of a man neither of us believe in. It's absurd.

CAROLINE: But for the fact that we're holding his money. He might come back just for the money. We'd be the first to meet him. 'Hello, here's your cheque.'

HENRY: Well, he never showed any interest in money before. Anyway, the fact that we're holding some money with his name on it doesn't make the possibility of his return any more likely. Does it?

CAROLINE: So you do regard it as a possibility?

HENRY: Ye . . . NO! (*Flummoxed*) I don't know. Give it to charity.

CAROLINE: (*Relentlessly*) But if we were wrong, we'd get it in the neck! We'd be singled out for divine retribution. (*Silence*)

HENRY: Look, this is silly! Forget it. Don't even *think* about it. (*He is obviously thinking furiously*) It's making me nervous.

CAROLINE: What about the money?

HENRY: Hmmn?

CAROLINE: (*Sharply*) Behind you!

HENRY: (*Whirling round to look at the door*) What?

CAROLINE: (*Laughing at him*) In the safe.

HENRY: (*Sighing with relief*) Oh. If it had Julius Caesar's name on it, would that mean that Julius Caesar was going to call round and pick it up?

CAROLINE: Julius Caesar never said he was going to come back, did he?

HENRY: (*Trying to reassure himself*) Look Caroline, do you honestly expect me to believe that Jesus Christ is going to turn up here?

CAROLINE: (*Casually referring to her notes*) 'The

Son of Man comes at a time you do not
expect.'

HENRY: Who said?

CAROLINE: Jesus. Matthew twenty-four, forty-four.

HENRY: Ah, but that means he could come back
at any old time. That's just to keep you
on your toes.

CAROLINE: (*Perching on the front of the desk*) Even
a conservative estimate gives him a fifty
per cent chance of speaking the truth.
Either he was or he wasn't.

HENRY: (*As if resting his case*) Take it or leave it.

CAROLINE: (*Reading from the gospel*) 'One will be
taken and the other left.' (*Pause*) Fifty
per cent chance there, too.

HENRY: (*After another pregnant pause*)
Nervous?

CAROLINE: How do we know that either of *us* will
be taken?

HENRY: Does the . . . um . . . does the Bible
give any clues?

(*Blackout. When this is not possible,
they freeze*)

APPENDIX ONE

Cross Reference to Sketches for
Special Occasions in *Time to Act*
(Hodder & Stoughton),
Lightning Sketches (Hodder & Stoughton)
and *Laughter in Heaven* (Marc Europe)

Most of these sketches are listed under the appropriate
headings without explanation – a few are directly con-
nected with a festival (New Year and Easter, for example),
but many are developments of a relevant theme.

ADVENT	'The Light of the World' (*TTA*), 'The Parable of the Ranch' (*TTA*).
CHRISTMAS	'Angel Space' (*LS*).
NEW YEAR	'Final Resolution' (*LIH*).
EPIPHANY	'Wisdom and Folly' (*TTA*).
WEEK OF CHRISTIAN UNITY	'An Eye for an Eye' (*LS*).
LENT	'Spreading the Word Around a Bit' (*LS*), 'Short Cut to Nowhere' (*LS*). (Both sketches take a hard look at attitudes and the need for repentance).
MOTHERING SUNDAY	'David and Goliath' (*LS*). (Cf. the decision to use a sketch for children and the theme of trusting in God, in *Red Letter Days*).
GOOD FRIDAY	'For the Good of the Team' (*LS*), 'Question Time' (*LS*).
EASTER	'Love and Death' (*TTA*), 'Early One Morning' (*LS*), 'Bodyguard' (*LIH*),

'Life is but a Melancholy Flower'
(*LIH*), 'The Trial of Trimmer Trend'
(*LIH*).

CHRISTIAN
AID WEEK
'One for Me and None for You' (*TTA*),
'The Appointment' (*TTA*), 'The
Widow's Mites' (*TTA*).

ASCENSION
'The Interrogation' (*LIH*). (This
dramatises some astonished reactions at
the healing of the centurion's servant,
showing the authority and power of
Jesus to act without being physically
present).

PENTECOST
'Importunity Knocks' (*TTA*), 'In the
Nick of Time' (*LS*), 'Do Unto Others'
(*LIH*). (For the significance of 'Do
Unto Others', cf. 'The Comforter' in
Red Letter Days).

TRINITY
'The Story of King Josiah' (*TTA*) (for a
children's sketch on the theme of a
biblical foundation for doctrine), 'The
Examination' (*LS*), 'Talking Heads'
(*LIH*) (for a treatment of the question,
'What is a Christian?').

HARVEST
THANKSGIVING
'The Parable of the Talents' (*TTA*).

ALL SAINTS
DAY
'How to be a Hero' (*LS*).

GUY FAWKES
NIGHT
'Prince of Peace' (*LS*).

REMEMBRANCE
SUNDAY
'Violence in the Home' (*TTA*) (how
war starts in the human heart).

MISSIONARY
SUNDAY
'The Parable of the Good Punk Rocker'
(*TTA*).

ADVENT II
'The Last Judgement' (*TTA*).

Other Occasions not Included in *Red Letter Days*

PALM SUNDAY
'Zacc's for Tax' (*LS*) (originally written
for children's Palm Sunday service).

BIBLE SUNDAY	'General Conformity' (*LS*).
FATHER'S DAY	'Importunity Knocks' (*TTA*) (especially the section dealing with fathers and children).
A WEDDING	'100% Proof' (*LIH*).
A BAPTISM	'Keep on Keeping on' (*TTA*) (for a look at John the Baptist and the message of repentance), 'David and Goliath' (*LS*) (for the theme of spiritual warfare), 'The Lost Sheep' in *Red Letter Days* (for the theme of following the Good Shepherd).

APPENDIX TWO

THE DEVELOPMENT OF THE WORK OF RIDING LIGHTS THEATRE COMPANY

In concluding the publication of yet another book of sketches, the authors have inevitably been asking themselves, 'Will this be the last?' The readership may well be asking the same question. Whether the answer is 'yes' or 'no', there is certainly a need to talk briefly about developments beyond the scope of such books, to counteract the notion that Christian involvement with theatre is primarily concerned with what can be accomplished within the five-minute sketch. By way of illustration, it is perhaps useful to speak from our own experience of trying to develop the work of Riding Lights through an initial phase when the company was best known for its biblical and satirical sketches. Not that our own work in this respect has had any particular significance compared with similar work by others, but that if it is true that we have largely been responsible for popularising the comic sketch within the Christian community, we would also like to show by example that we have always been deeply committed to the production of fuller and more searching kinds of work. Our experience may hopefully encourage others to experiment along similar lines.

Ever since it began in 1977, Riding Lights Theatre Company has always been concerned, directly and indirectly, with the reawakening of a strong dramatic tradition within and flowing from the life of the church. Some might say that the church has never lost its dramatic tradition, pointing to writers like T. S. Eliot and Christopher Fry in this century or to the number of Passion and Nativity plays produced annually by various congregations. But even they would have to concede that never before in the history of the church has so much theatre been performed by Christians on so many occasions in halls and churches, on beaches and streets, in youth clubs and theatres. Thousands of churches throughout the world now have official 'drama groups', in addition to choirs and rotas of 'sidespersons'. Many major church events now consider the possibility of including theatre in their programmes. (In 1982, the Roman Catholic church took the surprising step of inviting Riding Lights to perform for twenty minutes on the theme of 'Marriage and Family Life' to a vast crowd gathered on York race course, eagerly awaiting the arrival of the Pope by helicopter.) Hundreds of sketches are written for special occasions, missions and services; groups meet every week to rehearse; speakers and preachers now often welcome dramatic interludes to illustrate their talks and sermons.

The sheer volume of all this grassroots theatrical activity is without precedent, but like all new growth, it must strengthen and mature in order to survive or it will soon wither and die out. If a strong dramatic tradition is to be established, we must push ourselves beyond the easy and the 'throw-away' and strive to create work which, like a great oratorio or painting, will be perceived by both Christians and unbelievers to have some lasting value for its artistic excellence, its breadth, depth and meaning.

The two unusual characteristics of this resurgence of theatre already hinted at – the predominance of the sketch and the use of comedy – may be the result of some fairly obvious factors. On one level, sketches have been taken up so widely simply because they are easier to produce, they fit without undue disturbance into the existing structures (services, school assemblies, etc) and they neatly encapsulate a message or a story. In this way theatre can be introduced as a lively, new *ingredient*, rather than an activity which actors and audience pursue in its own right. The emergence of the sketch may also be a product of the times, of the revue-style television comedy of the sixties and seventies (an influence which Riding Lights would acknowledge), but this is unusual in the church context, since most of what had gone before was in terms of plays and verse-dramas. (Even the 'one-act' Mystery Plays were arranged in continuous cycles.) This trend is quite understandable in the early stages, even sensible from an educational point of view, though we must beware the sketch-form becoming a rut which will be increasingly narrow.

Sketches lead quite naturally to comedy and here again there is a break with religious tradition, or at least a rediscovery of a quality for which religious drama has not been particularly noted since the Middle Ages. It is a joyous thing that churches can now and again be filled with laughter, but it would be sad if this, too, became a stumbling-block to a greater variety of expression: as evidenced by the numbers of groups who have complained to us that 'they can't write funny sketches' and so feel inhibited about writing anything. Why *should* they feel compelled to write funny sketches? Although several of the sketches in this book are not particularly funny and all of them are examples of 'the serious business of comedy', part of the answer to this question lies in the fact that it is far harder to write, and far more difficult for an audience to receive, a totally serious *sketch*. Tragedy cannot be achieved in five minutes; if attempted, it will almost immediately become comedy anyway. There is no time for the audience to establish an emotional relationship with the characters and their predicament, so it is precisely at this point that the dramatist must reach out beyond the confines of the sketch and, if need be, avoid the 'tyranny' of trying to be funny. Riding Lights would never wish its own reputation to become a strait-jacket for others.

So much for the warnings, the technical observations and appearing to prune the very branch we're sitting on. Perhaps hindsight will show that the most original contribution ultimately made by Riding Lights to the annals of British theatre will be *The Parable of the Good Punk Rocker* and other transitory pieces in similar vein. We sincerely hope not. Doubtless, as with this current collection, sketches will continue to play an important part in the company's work and within the work of many other groups but we are sure that it is the other areas of our theatrical work which are capable of much greater development.

During the first phase of the company's life (1977–84), it always seemed to be a strength that the group could apply itself to so many different types of theatre; we were fortunate to be given such a variety of opportunities and such an adaptable company of actors and actresses. It was invigorating to chop and change between revue, classical plays, new plays, children's shows and musicals, between tragedy, farce, satire, theatre-in-education, between arts festivals, Christian festivals and pop festivals, to perform one week in a big proscenium-arch theatre, the next in a prison, a city square, a cathedral, a bar, a television studio, an arts centre or wherever. Different skills emerged and each type of work, each environment, gave something fresh to take on into the next project. Through no special gifts but rather through the harsher realities of experience, the company learnt how to survive in very adverse performing conditions, such as the notorious Edinburgh Festival Fringe Club, the graveyard for so many eager and nervous cabaret acts. In general, a large and fluctuating repertoire of both biblical and satirical sketches gave the company a stock-in-trade of infinitely variable shows to suit all occasions and invitations, which were constantly sandwiched between our fuller-length productions.

Initially, the work was built around the talents and personalities of a resident company of five or six actors for whom material could be specially written. With the minimum of props and sets, the work was highly flexible and comparatively mobile, depending on the state of the van. Our output fell broadly into three categories: major productions of plays and musicals, which were often commissioned from our own writers; the sketch repertoire providing 'made-to-measure' performances in a whole range of contexts; regular educational shows in the North Yorkshire community. All three areas developed side by side with little time for the company to become stale doing a particular show or one type of work. Had Riding Lights had its own theatre it would have been able to give greater shape to the diary, to have had firmer control over its touring schedule and, ultimately, would have been freer to pursue its major productions for longer periods. As it was, at least we were given the proverbial spice of life in fullest measure.

Since less is generally known about the first of the three categories outlined above, we have included a diary of the company's major productions over the years. There are about forty separate productions here, including some for television. They are listed, with occasional press reaction, partly for interest and partly to put the earlier discussion about the predominance of sketches into some kind of perspective.

Major Riding Lights Productions

1977   THE CONCISE BOOK OF FLUFFED LIONS
        (*revue at Queen's University, Belfast, Arts Festival*)
        THE LIGHTER SIDE OF THE MOON (*a trilogy
        of one-act plays by Murray Watts*)
        THE MIGHTY HUNTER (*play by Wolf
        Mankowicz*)
        GOD REST YOU MERRY (*Christmas play for
        young children by Nigel Forde and Murray Watts*)
1978   THE TRIAL OF TRIMMER TREND (*morality
        play by Murray Watts*)
        ALL FOOLS' NIGHT (*revue*)
        STUFF AND NONSENSE (*play for infants by
        Nigel Forde*)
        EVER BEEN 'AD? (*schools' show about
        advertising by Nigel Forde*)

THE COMPLETE WORKS (*revue-style show about poetry and poets, devised by Nigel Forde and presented to fifth and sixth forms*)

1979 A GENTLEMAN'S AGREEMENT (*co-production with Upstream Theatre Club of a new farce by Murray Watts*)

'New comedy hits its target . . . brought the house down last night.'

Yorkshire Evening Press

POSTMAN'S KNOCK (*play for young children by Nigel Forde, Paul Burbridge and Murray Watts*)

DANIEL (*muscial by Murray Watts and Christopher Norton produced in co-operation with singers, dancers, musicians and actors of St Michael-le-Belfrey church, York*)

'All round success. Many of the musical numbers would do credit to the West End stage.'

Yorkshire Evening Press

THE LAST DAY OF A CONDEMNED MAN (*one-man show, adapted and directed by Murray Watts from the story by Victor Hugo*)

'Brilliantly conceived.' *Time Out*

COLOUR RADIO (*the first of the Edinburgh Festival revues. Won a Fringe First Award from* The Scotsman *newspaper*)

'Riding Lights Theatre Company are outstanding. One of the most exciting revues on the Fringe this year.'

The Scotsman

A WINTER'S TALE (*Christmas show for children by Nigel Forde*)

1980 THE LOVE OF KING DAVID AND THE FAIRE BETHSABE (*Elizabethan play by George Peele, adapted by Paul Burbridge. Directed by Murray Watts and designed by Gill Douglas*)

'Peele's textbook reputation as an undramatic lyricist is here belied.'

The Observer

(Was that a good or bad review?)

GUY FAWKES NIGHT (*musical by Murray Watts and Christopher Norton premiered at the York Festival in co-operation with the congregation of St Michael-le-Belfrey church*)

> 'Guy Fawkes Night pleases its audience and is full of good things.'
>
> *The Daily Telegraph*

COLOUR RADIO II (*revue at the Edinburgh Festival*)

THE COMPLETE WORKS (*the poetry show revised and improved*)

(*With these two shows the company won The Charlie Parker Award for its work at the Edinburgh Festival*)

THE GRAND SLAM (*children's musical by Murray Watts and Christopher Norton, toured nationally for the Pathfinder organisation*)

GOD REST YOU MERRY (*Christmas play for primary schools*)

1981 CATWALK (*play about a Soviet dissident by Murray Watts. Toured to Holland in 1982 for Theatr de Blauwe Zaal*)

> 'A stark story, effectively brought to the stage in a very fine production. All six actors are individually accomplished and function outstandingly well as an ensemble.'
>
> *The Scotsman*

THE BEST OF COLOUR RADIO cassette (*live recording of revue at the Lyons Concert Hall, produced by Victor Lewis-Smith*)

COLOUR SUPPLEMENT (*Edinburgh Festival revue*)

THE SECRET (*musical for children by Paul Burbridge and Christopher Norton*)

ANGEL AT LARGE (*Christmas play by Nigel Forde, toured to primary schools in North Yorkshire*)

1982   THE ADVENTURES OF SIR SINGALOT (*play for infants by Vicky Ireland*)
       JONATHAN MARTIN (*play by Murray Watts about the nineteenth-century 'incendiary of York Minster', commissioned and filmed for Yorkshire TV. Directed by Alfredo Michelsen, produced by Nick Gray*)

> 'A moving and impressive piece. The Riding Lights Company adapts magnificently from stage to TV studio.'
>
> *Yorkshire Evening Press*

       THE BEST OF RIDING LIGHTS (*video of ten sketches for Trinity Video directed by Michael Hart*)
       KINGDOM RUN (*children's musical by Richard Everett and Dave Cooke*)
       A WINTER'S TALE (*Christmas show for children by Nigel Forde*)

1983   PROMISE (*play by Andrew Goreing*)
       THE GENTLE PATH (*play for younger children by Nigel Forde, toured nationally with Kingdom Run and Promise for C.P.A.S.*)
       HAPPY MEDIA (*revue for York summer season*)

> 'This is literary humour at its best . . . and has a good deal of bite.'
>
> *The Guardian*

       JONATHAN MARTIN (*stage version of the television play by Murray Watts*)
       THE COMPLETE WORKS (*the poetry show returns by popular demand*)

> 'A show to be recommended. Without being esoteric, it tickles the nose of the sleeping lion, English Literature. The wit is of a high order.'
>
> *Edinburgh Festival Times*

       IN CAMERA (*by Jean-Paul Sartre. A Workshop production*)
       THE VANITY CASE (*revue based on the book of Ecclesiastes by Paul Burbridge and Nigel Forde*)

> 'Comic invention that both instructs and

entertains is rare. It is this priceless commodity
that Riding Lights display in their latest
production.'

Buzz Magazine

ON CHRISTMAS NIGHT (*seasonal play for
young children by Nigel Forde*)

1984 THE VANITY CASE (*a further national tour*)
VERTICAL HOLD (*two-man revue*)

'Hilariously irreverent and topical look at the
hypocrisy and superficiality of the twentieth
century. The evening was a sheer delight.'

Yorkshire Evening Press

ST JOHN'S GOSPEL (*adapted and directed for the
stage by Murray Watts for the York Festival*)
MOSCOW CIRCLES (*one-man show based on the
underground novel by Benedict Erofeev, performed
by Alfredo Michelsen. Produced in conjunction
with Canto, directed by Murray Watts*)

'Brilliant theatrical success.'

Radio Television Eire

HOW FAR IS IT TO BETHLEHEM? (*Christmas
play by Nigel Forde for primary schools in North
Yorkshire*)

1985 ST JOHN'S GOSPEL (*nine-week tour to major
theatres in Scotland and England. Set designed by
Sean Cavanagh, costumes by Sally Scraggs*)

'A beautifully judged piece of theatre,
powerfully simple in its concept . . . The evening
is studded with illuminated moments . . . The
ancient plainchant echoes of "Come Holy
Ghost", which ends the performance, has a
magical beauty of sound which sends one away
with the realisation that here have been enacted
the elements of a simple belief, whose message
and strength are worth a dozen intellectually
enquiring sermons.'

Eastern Daily Press

W.A.R.P. (Worldwide Anglican Renewal Project)

(*satirical spoof documentary for Central
Television's 'Encounter' series*)
> 'A witty script hitting a variety of targets – not all
> of them sitting. This Encounter was something of
> a landmark.'
>
> *Church of England Newspaper*

THE MAIN POINTS AGAIN (*revue*)
THE MODEL WIFE and A FUNNY THING (*two
one-act plays by Murray Watts*)
IT SHOULD HAPPEN TO A DOG (*play by Wolf
Mankowicz, directed by Paul Burbridge*)
ST JOHN'S GOSPEL (*a remounted production for
a further tour in Wales and England*)
> 'An astonishing coup de théâtre.'
>
> *Yorkshire Post*

ANGEL AT LARGE (*Christmas play for children
by Nigel Forde*)

1986 THE PAGEANT OF THE RED AND WHITE
ROSES (*performed in York Minster, celebrating
the five hundredth anniversary of the union of the
Houses of Lancaster and York*)

Ten of the shows appearing in this diary represent the
company's work in the third category – educational shows
for the schools of North Yorkshire. The inspiration for
almost all of these came from the typewriter of one of the
company directors, Nigel Forde, whose plays and muscial
direction created a highly popular local tradition amongst
the Top Junior age-group, particularly at Christmas time.
Five of the shows successfully blended the nativity theme
with hilarious elements of pantomime, to the delight of
thousands of children and teachers throughout the country.
The chance to work from home to such enthusiastic response has always had a special attraction year by year.

The sketch repertoire led the company into two main
areas of work. Four major revues, full of satire, wit and
silliness, established the company's name on the Edinburgh
Festival Fringe. These reappeared in various guises and

combinations in many other theatres. The other strand of sketch was, of course, the biblical one, or the one geared to the presentation of some aspect of Christian experience and teaching. The production of much of this material came out of a close working relationship with the evangelist David Watson who, between 1977 and 1982, 'rarely spoke without a sketch'. With him, the company took part in numerous city-wide Christian Festivals: Belfast, Leeds, Manchester, Newcastle, Cornwall, London, Bournemouth and Birmingham. Sometimes the stages would be as huge as the Albert Hall or the Barbican Centre; sometimes as unusual as Crumlin Road Jail or Wensleydale cheese factory. During our final major engagement with David in 1982, over a period of nineteen days in London, we calculated that we performed a hundred and twenty-one sketches, fifty-nine of these were different and only nine of them could be classed as 'revue' sketches! Is it any wonder why people thought we never did anything else? The contribution of theatre became such a vital part of David Watson's ministry, that when Riding Lights were unable to accompany him because of the demands of our other productions, he put together a team of actors, dancers and musicians who continued to perform the material all over the world. Despite the stresses and strains of this mission work, it was so good to see the entertaining and communicating power of theatre working effectively in the cause of the Christian gospel.

In the second phase of the company's development, from 1984 onwards, the major change came with the disbanding of the resident company. Hard though this was, it was a necessary step to take, clearing the way for a different kind of creative energy, which was now coming from a production management, guided by the original directorship of the old company. While the working relationships forged in the early years will never be eclipsed, the thirty-five or so actors, actresses and technicians who have joined us for different productions over the last two years have been an enrichment to the life of the company. Another benefit of this change has been the freedom to extend the life of a successful production. 1985 virtually became the year of *St John's Gospel*, as the production toured both in the spring and in the autumn to twenty major theatres around Britain. It is further in this direction that the company is now attempting to move.

As far as exerting a significant influence within the mainstream of theatre and cultural life, little or nothing has yet been achieved. The most one can say is that foundations have been laid, not just by Riding Lights but by many other individual Christian artists and several other substantial initiatives such as the Arts Centre Group, Upstream Theatre Club, Aldersgate Productions, Footprints, Cornerstone and Back to Back theatre companies, Primary Colours and Direction Mime, to name but some.

If all our hopes for a strong dramatic tradition *flowing out* from the church are to come to any widely recognised fruition over the next few years, then it will be because three things have been firmly harnessed together. Prayer for the continued guidance and inspiration of the Holy Spirit. Tireless creativity from every individual artist. Committed and generous patronage from those in the church and in business who are in a position to allow this work to see the light of day. With this combination there is no reason why the future should not see many inroads being made into the darkness of our culture, bringing the fragrance of Christ to change the atmosphere. As actors and audience, we owe it to our society to press forward, for as Jesus said, 'Nobody lights a lamp and puts it under a bucket. They put it on a lampstand and it gives light to everyone.'

CHRISTIANITY AND THE THEATRE

There are many articles, both practical and theoretical, in TIME TO ACT and LIGHTNING SKETCHES, for those seeking to develop the art of performing sketches as an expression of Christian belief. For those wishing to look beyond the sketch, as the above appendix encourages, there is a special booklet written by Murray Watts, CHRISTIANITY AND THE THEATRE. Articles include the history of church and theatre, a theological response to some of the objections to theatre found in various traditions, an over-view of twentieth-century theatre and its role in society, censorship, patronage of the arts from within the church, and a history of some of the Christian companies and initiatives in recent times.

CHRISTIANITY AND THE THEATRE, published by the Handsel Press, should be available from your local bookshop. In case of difficulty, it can be ordered directly from the Handsel Press, 33 Montgomery St, Edinburgh EH7 5JX.